Retrain Your Brain
HEALING TRAUMA

CAROL CHARLAND

DEDICATION

To My Grandson, Liam

To my littlest one, your smiles and laughter brings me such joy. May you know all the blessings and treasures in life. Love you to the moon and back! Meme xoxo

Table of Contents

A Message From The Author

"To change the printout of the body, you must learn to rewrite the software of the mind" -Deepak Chopra

Retrain Your Brain HEALING TRAUMA is the beginning of the rest of your life. The 14 day program is unique, unlike other therapeutic programs you have tried in the past. It uses proven techniques that you can perform on yourself to break the emotional links deeply encoded in the brain associated with any stressful or traumatic event. It is not cognitive "talk" therapy and there is no pharmaceuticals for negative drug reactions. Most importantly, there is no need to re-live the traumatic event. The techniques you will learn seek out the emotion and symptom that has been deeply encoded in the brain connected to the event and dismantles it, completely and permanently, in a process called depotentiation. Anyone of any age can learn and easily perform these healing techniques for themselves.

If you suffer with symptoms of PTSD, post-covid stress, anxiety, depression, unexplained mood swings, hypervigilance, unresolved anger or resentment, grief, stress related insomnia, fatigue or unresolved post-injury pain syndromes from injuries that did not heal this book is meant for you.

Depotentiation is a process that literally seeks out the symptom(s) to the related event and dismantles it – completely. You will find that it not only heals the trauma but other unexplained symptoms like fatigue, insomnia, digestive issues, headaches may simply be eliminated as the depotentiation process in the brain unlinks symptoms to not only one specific traumatic event but all encoded trauma in general. You will find symptom(s) that have plagued you for years are completely resolved as the brain de-links all encoded trauma(s).

When you learn how the brain encodes trauma and the process it uses in depotentiation to release trauma symptoms, you will understand why other therapies you have tried failed in the past. Once the memory of the event is encoded it will remain so in spite of attempts to change it through controlling our emotions, cognitive talk therapy or masking symptoms with pharmaceuticals. The trauma is so deeply ingrained only psychosensory input can root it out to release it.

Healing Trauma is a 14 day program designed to empower YOU to take back control of your life and your health. You'll release stress and trauma encoded and stored in the brain, learn natural techniques to help you control stress and build emotional resiliency so that you are not prone to future trauma encoding, and finally you will learn specific techniques to help you regain self-confidence, self-esteem and set new goals so you can start living life to the fullest again.

I am not a professionally trained writer. I am a professionally trained NLP Neurolinguistics Practitioner that has successfully helped people achieve wellness goals since 1998. I use an easy-going conversational writing style as if you were a client sitting in my therapy office. The book is designed to be an instructional tool that teaches you powerful techniques for healing trauma and regaining a happy healthy life.

I intentionally made the book short in length, easy to read and understand. Instead of overwhelming you with medical terminology, it uses everyday terms. The chapters are set up as learning modules with step-by-step guides that teach you powerful Neurolinguistics techniques that you can start using immediately to reduce the symptoms of stress and trauma.

The Latest Cutting-Edge Therapy

Recordable Therapy Scripts are the latest innovative therapy. They have become the breakthrough therapy in retraining the brain programs. The meditation style scripts are written specifically with techniques that release old, encoded trauma stuck in the brain and create new neuropathways that help you achieve the positive behavioral change that you desire. The Recordable Therapy Scripts are a relaxing Medical Guided Imagery Meditations that incorporates powerful Neurolinguistics Techniques to "reframe" in the subconscious mind how you experience stress and trauma. The Scripts reinforce the permanent changes you obtain by using the neuroplasticity techniques.

Recordable Scripts are written scripts you read and record in your own voice. They are much more effective than listening to a pre-recorded audio that you purchase using a stranger's voice. You will be recording the therapy script in your own voice on your mobile phone memo recorder, computer or any recording device. Do not worry the recording instructions are fast and easy to do. Your subconscious mind relaxes as it recognizes your own voice on the recording and therefore, acts upon the therapy suggestions immediately and without hesitation. The therapeutic benefits start immediately. You simply let the relaxing guided imagery meditation infused with therapeutic suggestions fill your mind, brain and body with healing messages.

The Power of Neuroplastic Healing

One of the most exciting developments in medical research for treating trauma related issues is in the field of Neuroscience. Dr Norman Doidge MD's discovery in Neuroplasticity or how the brain is constantly changing and easily "unlearns" old behavior patterns including those associated with stress and trauma has become the foundation of revolutionary new treatment programs like *Healing Trauma*. His discovery in Neuroplasticity proves it is possible to change dysfunctional patterns of thinking and behaving into new more positive behaviors.

Neuroplasticity is defined as the brain's ability to grow and evolve in response to life experiences. The brain is a dynamic organ that is always changing and remolding itself by reorganizing neural connections, often referred to as "wiring or rewiring" of the brain. Neuroscientists refer to this process as structural remodeling of the brain.

The brain changes behavior patterns overtime by creating new neurons and building new neuropathways. The most amazing fact of this discovery is that learning a few simple mind-body techniques that you perform on yourself can help rewire responses once thought to be permanently deep-rooted or encoded in the brain. The key to building new neural pathways is as simple as repetition of a specific technique or activity. You simply repeatedly practice the new technique for the change you desire so it becomes the new neuropathway ingrained in the brain.

The techniques you will learn in *Healing Trauma* are revolutionary methods evolved from the discoveries in neuroplasticity. Traumas once thought to be deeply ingrained in the brain and unchangeable are quickly released without re-living the traumatic event. You may be simply amazed, at the fast, positive results you obtain with these techniques.

We never truly know the power of the mind and body to heal itself until we give it the correct tools to be successful

 **You Hold The Key To Your Success**

Like anything in life, you get out of this program exactly what you put into it. Neural retraining is not difficult, but it does take consistent follow-through using the techniques repetitively to pave new neuropathways.

Following the instructions to the 14 day plan completely is needed to successfully obtain the benefits you desire. You will find that once you master the *Retrain Your Brain* techniques found in the book, you can use them to achieve many other goals in life.

What Is Trauma

Trauma comes from the Greek word for *wound*. Originally the word trauma was only used for physical wounds or injuries, over the years the definition has come to include emotional wounds. Trauma can leave psychological symptoms long after any physical injuries from an event have healed.

Trauma is defined as an emotional state resulting from experiencing a severe emotional event that is inescapable and overwhelming to comprehend. The psychological reaction to emotional trauma has an established name; PTSD or pos-traumatic stress disorder. Once thought to only occur after an extremely stressful event such as wartime combat, a natural disaster, from sexual or physical abuse, a traumatic accident or injury.

We now know if the landscape of the brain and other components are in place, stressful life events such as loss of a loved one, divorce, loss of career or job, diagnosis of incurable illness and many other stressful life experiences can be encoded in the brain and elicit the same trauma symptoms.

Types Of Traumas

Acute Trauma is intense distress in the aftermath of a one-time event common examples would be a car accident or the sudden death of a loved one.

Chronic Trauma can arise from harmful events that are repeated or prolonged it can develop in response to persistent abuse, bullying, neglect and domestic violence.

Complex Trauma arises from repeated experiences or multiple traumatic events from which there is no possibility of escape. It can undermine a sense of personal safety and security.

Vicarious Trauma arises from prolonged exposure to other people's suffering. It involves those in professions that are called on to respond to injury, natural disasters and mayhem. It is seen in the medical community, nurses and doctors, the military, first responders and law enforcement. The trauma symptoms experienced from vicarious trauma is known as compassion fatigue. The person emotionally shuts down, avoids investing emotionally in other people in an attempt to protect themselves from experiencing the distress seen in others.

Adverse Childhood Experiences includes children before they develop effective coping skills. It can be anything from a loss of a parent, neglect, physical or sexual abuse, divorce, being constantly moved or uprooted, perceived lack of security and safety.

Traumatization or the permanent encoding of a threatening event leads to many behavioral and cognitive disorders that include phobias, panic, post-traumatic stress and chronic pain it also increases the risk for other problems including substance abuse, depression, obesity, insomnia and other stress related disorders.

Very few people can go through their entire life without experiencing some stressful or traumatic event. Stress is very individual experience. People handle stress in their own way, they develop coping mechanisms that either make them stress hardy or make the landscape of the brain (potentiation) prone to encoding the stress permanently as trauma resulting in emotional and physical symptoms.

Most people have no way of knowing what stressful event or trauma has actually been encoded in the brain. They may develop unexplained symptoms like fatigue, headaches, insomnia depression, anxiety or panic and not ever relate it to encoded stress or trauma.

How Is Trauma Encoded

We now know that there are specific factors in how the brain encodes or stores traumatic events. Encoding of a trauma occurs as a result of potentiation or when all conditions come together simultaneously. In medical terms potentiation is defined as the ability to strengthen and augment a physiologically process synergistically.

Components Must Be Met For Traumatic Event:

1. The event must have meaning for the individual.
2. It produces intense emotion.
3. The landscape of the brain at the time of the event is reflected in one's low resiliency or vulnerability to traumatization
4. There is a perceived inescapability of the event in the moment it happens. The individual does not see a way out- there is no escape. (If an escape can be seen at that moment, traumatization does not get stored in the brain)

When a traumatic event is encoded it also encodes other components of the event.

Components Of A Traumatic Memory Are:

- Emotions: emotions experienced by the event
- Physical body: Autonomic Nervous System sensations generated in the body at the time of the event
- Cognitive Thinking: both conscious and subconscious aspects are involved

You may have many stressful events encoded in the brain that you are unaware. Traumatization occurs under certain conditions during a specific event. These events can be first hand, second hand or even third hand accounts as long as the mind can view the event, it has the potential to produce encoded traumatization.

When symptoms of stress or trauma arise it can feel like you've been swept up into an emotional rollercoaster ride, but you don't have to let it take over your life. With a   simple neural retraining technique,   so easy even children can do it   for themselves, you can calm yourself and wash away the symptoms of stress and trauma. You can even eliminate encoded events that you are unaware that may be causing symptoms.

In Module 4 you will learn this revolutionary life-changing technique. You can take back control and regain your life.

Stress Trauma and the Covid-19 Pandemic

Post Covid-19 Stress Disorder

The Covid-19 Pandemic has taken an emotional toll as well as physical on people around the world causing trauma like symptoms from pro-longed stress, uncertainty, anxiety and fear. With the outbreak came global mass hysteria where everyone's life was impacted by the uncertainty of the pandemic in some way.

As the vaccine is distributed and restrictions are lifted, people are now experiencing symptoms of post-traumatic stress disorder. You may have felt that you were coping well with the imposed life changes only to now once the threat has subsided are experiencing anxiety and unexplained symptoms. This condition has been labeled post-covid stress disorder.

A study published by CNN Network in February 2021 found that 30% of Covid-19 survivors in the USA were experiencing post-covid stress disorder or PTSD symptoms usually found in people surviving a life threatening experience. This figure does not include people experiencing PTSD symptoms from the fear of contracting the virus, economic hardships, deaths of family or friends, loss of job or from the many imposed life changes brought on by the pandemic.

Covid has lead to diverse mental health problems including anxiety, depression and post-traumatic stress disorder. Individuals working in a wide range of occupations have been negatively impacted however highly exposed individuals in the medical field: personnel, health care workers, first-responders, pharmacists, medical examiners and even in law enforcement that witnessed suffering, multiple deaths, death after heroic attempts to save people, making life and death decisions for sick people over such a prolonged period of time have been severely traumatized.

Traumatic Stressors

- Combating a severe illness
- Fear of contracting the virus
- Hospitalization
- Witnessing death (hearing of deaths)
- Death of a loved one
- Constant or inescapable exposure to COVID-19
- Media generated mass hysteria

Individual Stressors

- COVID-19 exposure or living under quarantine
- Social isolation
- Loss of income/ employment
- Working from home with kids/ lack of childcare
- Being a caregiver
- Making difficult medical decisions for loved ones
- Constant wearing of masks
- Work related burn-out
- Other individual life changes brought on by the pandemic

Post-Covid Stress Symptoms

- Emotional distress, anxiety, irrational fears, panic attacks
- Headaches
- Insomnia
- Fatigue, malaise, lethargy
- Depression, mood swings,
- Unexplained emotional outburst
- Substance use/abuse to cop

If you are experiencing symptoms of post-pandemic stress, you can use the neural retraining techniques in this program to relieve the emotions and stress related symptoms. You will find a calming, safe and transformative way to ease symptoms of Post-Covid Stress Disorder.

Medical Disclaimer

Please check with your doctor before making changes to your current medical care or starting any new health care regimen.

This book is not intended to diagnosis medical conditions. It is not meant to replace traditional medical care by your doctor or therapist. The author of this book does not dispense medical advice or the use of any of the techniques found in this book without the advice of your physician.

The intent of the author is only to share information of a general nature on neurolinguistic techniques already held in public knowledge. There is no implied guarantee for individual outcomes. In the event you use the information in this book for yourself, the author assumes no guarantees or responsibility for outcomes.

Note: Never use neurolinguistic pain management techniques for chest pain, heart or cardiac issues, abdominal pain or sudden onset of pain. These conditions can be a serious medical emergency and you should seek immediate medical attention.

Important Warning: Do not listen to the Recordable Meditation Script audio recordings while driving the car or doing any activity that requires your alert attention. Meditation type audio recordings can make you drowsy, they may distract you causing accidents. NLP, guided imagery visualizations and meditations can make you sleepy. They have the most benefit when used in a quiet relaxed setting.

Module 1: Introduction To Modern Neuroscience

This program is meant to empower you to achieve your wellness goals by giving you the tools you need to successfully change old, outdated behavior patterns related to stress and trauma. Neuroplastic healing gives you everything you need to release old messaging encoded or stuck in the brain and to create new healthy neuropathways for better health.

You will be using my revolutionary new 4R's System of Release-Reframe-Retrain-Restore wellness. I combined my expertise as a Clinical Hypnotherapist and CAM Complementary-Alternative Medicine - Neurolinguistics Practitioner with the latest medical findings in neuroscience on how the brain "unlearns" behavioral patterns and habits… including trauma patterns.

I have a remarkably high success rate helping people achieve their personal and wellness goals using these same techniques… and you can achieve this success too.

Rewiring or retraining the brain may sound complicated, but it is not. It is actually quite easy to learn and do. Most people find it relaxing and enjoyable. Plus, you will be learning NLP Neurolinguistic skills that can help you achieve other goals in life.

Discovering The Hidden Power Of The Brain

I always had an interest in the power of the mind and why people do what they do. When I was younger, I studied the works of Dale Carnegie and Norman Vincent Peale's power of positive thinking and using positive affirmations to affect personal life change.

My interest in the subconscious mind and mind-body medicine came later in 1990's when it was labeled "new age" and there was not a lot of medical research and science to validate it. Neuroscientist, Dr Candace Pert, MD changed that with her Nobel Prize-winning discovery on how emotions stored in the cells of the body can direct body function. She authored the books *"Molecules of Emotion"* and *"Your Body Is Your Subconscious Mind."*

NLP Neurolinguistics Programming was founded in the 1970's by Richard Bandler and John Grinder. The foundation of Neurolinguistics is language usage and how our mind and brain perceive words. In the beginning, NLP Neurolinguistics Programming was primarily used in psychotherapy counseling and for personal success development. Today it is the innovator for modern Neuroscience discoveries in how we retrain the brain to effect personal change in our lives.

We now have multiple research studies in Neuroscience that proves that our thoughts, the words we speak, and our emotions influence the chemistry and function of our mind and bodies. Dr Pert's discovery catapulted medical research and public interest into the mind-body connection.

We know from famous researchers like Dr Larry Dossey MD's books *"Healing Words; The Power of Prayer & The Practice of Medicine"* and *"Healing Beyond The Body: Medicine & The Infinite Reach of The Mind"* that the words we think and the words we speak are extremely powerful and have a way of directing the mind-brain-body even when we are unaware of it. Dr Dossey's work proves it is important to think and say the good words when we are in a healing phase. Our mind, brain and body are listening.

New discoveries in the field of Neuroscience have proven that it is possible that by choosing specific "words and phrases" to address specific problems in our lives, we can rewire our brains to help break through behavioral blocks, solve problems and even heal our body of pain and illness. The work of Dr Norman Doidge MD's work in Neuroplasticity of the brain *"The Brains Way Of Healing"* that it is flexible, ever-changing and can be rewired to "unlearn" certain behavior patterns, including stress, chronic pain and illness. You now have the power to change old "stuck" behavior patterns once believed to be permanent or unchangeable

Dr Andrew Newberg MD, a Neuroscientist at Thomas Jefferson University and Mark Waldman a communication expert, collaborated on a book "*Words Can Change Your Brain.*" In it, they write "a single word has the power to influence the expression of genes that regulate physical and emotional stress." When we use words filled with positivity like "love and peace" we can alter how our brain functions by increasing cognitive reasoning and strengthening areas in our frontal lobes, using positive words more often than negative ones can kickstart the motivational centers of the brain, propelling them into action.

Dr Newberg's discoveries goes much further than just the mind-body connection but in how the words we speak can actually change how the brain perceives reality or what is real from unreal. By holding a positive optimistic word or image in your mind, you stimulate frontal lobe activity. This area includes specific language centers that connect directly to the motor cortex responsible for moving you into action, and as research has shown, the longer you concentrate on positive words and images, the more you begin to affect other areas of the brain. Functions in the frontal lobe start to change, which changes your perception of yourself to a more positive perception of yourself and your abilities. He writes "Overtime the structure of your thalamus will also change in response to your conscious words, thoughts and feelings. We believe that the thalamic changes affect the way in which you perceive reality."

You will learn an immensely powerful NLP technique called Role Modeling as one of the tools of the 4R's System. It uses Dr Newberg's discoveries in changing the internal image or perception of yourself to one that is healthier, free of trauma symptoms, pain or discomfort so you can easily achieve your set wellness goal.

Later in the book you will learn more about the power of the subconscious mind and how it can help you achieve goals. The subconscious, like a computer data system has no mechanism to determine real from unreal. As Dr Newberg's research has proven, an image of a juicy tart lemon can be as real to the subconscious mind as if you were holding a real lemon in your hand.

NLP Neurolinguistics is no longer "new age phenomenon" it is proven to be effective in the latest discoveries in the field of neuroscience. New research discoveries in Neuroscience in brain neuroplasticity is the foundation of this NLP Neurolinguistic program and my 4R's Neuroplastic Healing System. The techniques you will be taught in this book are scientifically proven effective for healing trauma.

Module 2: Change Your Brain ~ Change Your Life

Modern Discoveries In Brain Neuroplasticity

Neuroscientists have proven that your brain is constantly being shaped and molded by life's everyday experiences. Your brain is influenced daily by what is happening in your life. This one single scientific breakthrough in brain neuroplasticity has greatly changed the way we approach how we change unwanted behaviors and habits even ones thought unchangeable. Every thought you think and feeling you feel, strengthens the circuitry in your brain known as your neural pathways.

Neural pathways are the foundation of your habits of thinking, feeling, and acting. They are what you believe to be true and why you do what you do. Using techniques such as NLP Neurolinguistics to rewire or retrain the brain has the ability to transform our mind and bodies by mobilizing our thoughts and practicing new ways of thinking, acting and feeling.

Research into Neuroplastic healing has proven that we can mold our nerve cell network and literally change how our brains work by changing neuropathways.

Every positive thought you think and words you speak reinforce the changes you desire and strengthens the brain's electrical grid or nerve circuitry known as neural pathways. Changing an old habit and forging a new neuropathway for positive change involves hundreds of millions of interwoven connections between nerve cells and nerve pathways. This pathway then becomes part of the mind-brain-body connection.

Forging New Neural Pathways For Change

I like to describe the intricate neural circuitry in the brain that forms neural pathways as a maze of interconnected walking paths or trails through the woods. The more you repeatedly travel the same trail over and over again, clearing away the debris or obstacles, the stronger and more permanently embedded the pathway becomes. When you repeatedly travel down these new neural pathways using new behaviors (NLP techniques), the old unused path begins to fade away. The most used path will become the strongest. It will become the default setting in the mind's master computer and be used first before a weaker less prominent one. Like walking the same wooded trail, by repeatedly practicing the NLP techniques, you are paving new neural pathways that the brain will set as a "default path" automatically following the new behavior. Repetition of the NLP techniques is key to successfully achieving your goals.

This new behavior or habit formation is dependent on repeatedly training our brain to create the new pathway. Some people see immediate results, for some it may take days or even weeks to notice a lessening of symptoms, but do not quit the program. For some deeply ingrained habits, it can take up to 21 days for the brain to switch gears when changing habits. Follow the daily program instructions completely, repeatedly practice the techniques given to create new neural pathways and you will see the results you desire.

The Mind-Brain Body Connection

What we used to think of as the mind-body connection, we now know is actually the mind-brain-body connection. Your mind, brain and body are intricately connected together in a circuitry system of interwoven nerves and neural pathways that dictate behaviors; how you act, feel and think.

Activate Neurons And Open New Pathways

Repetition reinforcing the new behavior forges the new pathway. Positive feelings and emotions activate neurons and open the pathways. The more intense the positive feelings the more neurons are activated solidifying the neural pathway. Feelings and emotions act as the glue that binds you to the new behavior or pathway.

Neural pathways are reinforced into habits through the repetition of intentionally thinking, feeling and acting full of emotion in the new chosen behavior. Later in the book you will learn the NLP Role Modeling Technique. This is a powerful tool to build new neural pathways. Using visualization techniques and the NLP Role Modeling technique you will build new pathways to successful change. As you daydream and visualize yourself healed, healthy and successfully achieving your goals, make the visualization bold, vivid and beautiful, full of positive emotion that activates the neurons and solidifies the new behavior. Remember to use the same imagery and visualization every day to strengthen and solidify the neural path.

Retraining The Brain

The 4R's Neuro-healing System rewires your brain from old, outdated behavior patterns. It helps change your symptoms by releasing the root cause of why your mind-brain-body ever developed it. Reversing the steps of how the brain creates a behavioral pattern or habit forges new neuropathways (behavior patterns), so you experience relief of symptoms.

First of all, it does not matter if you have had these symptoms for one month or all of your life. This program can help you. The subconscious mind has no time consciousness. It either knows you have these specific symptoms, or you do not. You will be creating new neural pathways for relief. If you have tried different methods to relieve your symptoms but have failed or even if you are hesitant in believing this program will work for you, if you follow this program completely, you should notice a significant change in symptoms. You simply have to follow the program instructions completely; repeatedly do the practice NLP techniques as instructed and listen to the therapeutic recordable meditation script consistently.

The Subconscious Mind

This program is unlike any other; you will be using a part of your mind called the subconscious mind. There is the conscious and subconscious mind(s) that we use in retraining the brain. When you are awake, you use the alert conscious "common sense" mind to filter information. When you relax and sleep, the alert, filtered mind relaxes, it is turned off and the subconscious mind becomes dominant.

You open the doorway to the subconscious mind when you relax, daydream and sleep. When you work with the subconscious mind you are tapping into the immensely powerful mind-brain-body connection where the mind instructs the body.

Understanding how the subconscious works will help you to better understand how this program can help you take back control of your life from the grip of trauma.

Rewire The Master Computer In Your Brain

NLP Neurolinguistic techniques are the tools we use to retrain the brain or reset the master computer in the subconscious mind. The subconscious mind functions like a master computer; that runs off from a software program, it stores all information in your memory from the moment you were born, even though your conscious alert mind does not remember things, the subconscious mind does remember. The subconscious holds memory of the traumatic event, and the emotions associated with it.

The master computer is running off from a software program made up of old neuro-pathways or behavior patterns, much like a database in a computer it can be re-programmed to perform different functions and create new behavior patterns and habits.

Just like a computer, the subconscious mind's master computer has no mechanism to determine real from unreal; it simply gathers information, stores it memory and acts upon the programming. It never shuts off and is always taking in information and filing it away in your memory forming neural pathways. It even stores information of which you are unaware.

The ability to use modern NLP Neurolinguistic techniques to successfully tap into the subconscious mind is what allows the retraining of the brain to change behavior patterns creating new neuropathways in the brain.

Why You Have Failed At Changing Trauma Symptoms In The Past

Most behaviors patterns come from a software package installed in this master computer in your brain a long time ago, going back to when you were a child. If you feel your symptoms come from a specific injury or trauma (psychological or physical trauma) this system can re-program the master computer in your subconscious mind releasing all of the old programming including chronic pain and trauma related symptoms.

In the past, when you have tried to change habits, your subconscious mind was still programmed to the old way of thinking. No one ever deleted the old software program (the encoded trauma in the brain) in the master computer. Utilizing the powerful NLP Neuroscience techniques, you are able to communicate directly with your subconscious mind to release and delete the old programming that has been stuck in the subconscious mind all the way back to when the traumatic event happened, and symptoms first developed.

When the master computer in your subconscious mind replaces the old data software with healthy habits you desire, that is exactly what you get. Your subconscious mind already knows how to do this. It holds in its memory what it is like to be free of trauma, to be healthy, and to be well.

Affirmation For Creating A Neural Pathway: *"I act, feel and think like a calm, healthy, happy, person would act, feel and think… as if, I have always been calm healthy, happy and free of trauma"*

Like a computer, when you delete the outdated programming in the subconscious, the new changes are immediate. It simply acts on the new programming just like a computer would when re-programmed to perform a different action. Most people notice an immediate change in behaviors and habits that gets stronger as you repeatedly practice the NLP Neurolinguistics techniques.

Oftentimes, in my therapy practice, I hear a client say, "I have no self-discipline to stick with things, I just don't have any willpower, will this still work for me?" The answer is yes, it will. Unlike other systems, this one is not based on willpower; it is based on releasing the old outdated neural pathways and creating new neural paths re-programming the information stored in the subconscious mind. We are simply undoing all the symptoms related to a stored trauma memory on the master computer of your mind. It is as simple as clicking a "delete" key to delete old software programs on a computer and then installing new software.

Learning more about the subconscious mind allows you to understand how this all works to help you achieve your wellness goal and can help you to create new neural pathways to achieve many other goals in life.

- You can access the subconscious mind through a state of relaxation, daydreaming, meditation, trance or sleep. So, when you use programs like this one, no deep trance state is needed… only relaxation.

- Like a computer, it has no mechanism to tell real from unreal. Words and images can be very real to the subconscious mind. Dr Andrew Newberg's research findings validate that using the "right words" has the ability to change our perception of life and reality.

- It has no time consciousness

- It is dominant when you are relaxed or sleeping

- The language of the subconscious mind is pictures and symbols; it is how you talk to it and instruct it. Remember, it has no mechanism to tell real from unreal.

- When you dream and see vivid images and symbols, it is the subconscious talking to you in its own language through pictures and symbols in your dream.

- We use NLP Neurolinguistics (words, phrases, metaphors) guided imagery meditations, visualization of symbols to instruct the subconscious mind to take action.

- We use these NLP techniques to tap into the mind-brain-body connection in order to instruct it and get the response we desire.

- Like a computer running on a software program, your subconscious mind acts on words, suggestions and images when told to do so.

- The subconscious mind is very literal, what you feed it… is what you get.

- NLP Neurolinguistics is not hypnosis; no deep trance state is needed to be successful.

KEY: Remember we are dealing with the subconscious mind, not the conscious waking mind. The subconscious does not work off from time or age. It does not even have a mechanism to tell it real from unreal. These NLP techniques simply reverse the stages of how the brain created the behavior pattern (symptom of trauma) and pushes the "delete key" on that outdated software program.

Module 3: Mind-Body Tools For Retraining The Brain

The 4R's System

The 4 R's Neuro-healing System of release, reframe, retrain and restore wellness teaches you these new, easy to learn techniques. You release symptoms associated with stress and trauma being sent to the brain, reframe how you experience stressful events and retrain the neuropathways of the brain using modern techniques in neuroplasticity to restore your health and wellness.

The 4R's System uses modern NLP Neurolinguistics Techniques and therapeutic Guided Imagery Meditations that taps into the mind-brain-body connection to communicate with the master computer in the subconscious mind. It retrains the brain by deleting old, outdated neural programming in the subconscious mind, it is like clicking the delete key on a computer program and installing new information to create new neuropathways that develop into new positive behaviors.

What Is Reframing

The 4R's System uses a powerful NLP technique called Reframing. Reframing is a term used in psychology to change the way you think about something, thus changing how you experience it. Reframing has the power to change your mental perspectives and how you experience "things" in life, including how you experience stress, trauma and chronic pain. It can make a traumatic injury or stressful event less traumatic. In the same regard, when used for healing trauma, reframing techniques have the power to change how you experience symptoms related to a stressful traumatic event. It can change negative beliefs like; nothing helps me, I cannot overcome this. It is an immensely powerful technique that can be used to turn a negative experience into a more positive perspective of the event.

What Is NLP Neurolinguistics

NLP commonly known as Neurolinguistic Programming is based in psychology, it uses special communication techniques to change people's thoughts and behaviors. NLP operates through the "conscious" use of language to bring about changes in someone's thoughts and behavior. NLP has been widely used by psychologist for phobias, depression, anxiety, PTSD and proven highly effective. Studies have proven there are numerous benefits of using NLP, for example, a study published in the *Journal of Counseling and Psychotherapy Research* found patients had improved symptoms and improved quality of life after having NLP Neurolinguistics therapy.

Neurolinguistics is the study of how the language we speak is processed in the human brain. How the brain interprets information, stores it in memory and then implements it to create certain actions or behaviors. It is founded on the idea that people operate by internal "maps" of the world that they learned through their own childhood upbringing and personal experiences. Not every person experiences the same life events in the same way, it is a very individual process, it is our life experiences that give us our beliefs and unique perspective of things. Traumatic events is also very individual experience. What is traumatic for one person may not be for another. People experience traumatic events differently based upon their internal beliefs. NLP Neurolinguistics Techniques help retrain the brain by influencing how the brain processes and encodes or stores the information it is given.

Mind-Body Tools For Retraining The Brain

Medical Guided Imagery is a mind-body tool used in retraining the brain. You have heard of imagery or visualization work, much like daydreaming where you simply picture an image in your mind. Medical Guided Imagery uses medical terminology to tap into the mind-brain-body connection using symbols, images, and verbal suggestions to instruct the body to perform a certain behavior to enhance or change your health. It uses medical knowledge of how the body functions to instruct the mind-brain-body through symbols and verbal suggestions. For example, you may picture the symbol of a dial like the one used for the pain scale to represent your level of pain by manipulating the numbers on the dial turning the dial down to a lower number, you can help lower pain levels. Medical Guided Imagery can be an effective therapy for a wide variety of health conditions.

The medical terminology and symbols in the imagery are intertwined in a relaxing guided meditation with visions of a warm sandy beach to achieve your wellness goals. Think of Medical Imagery as a special code to talk to the body. It can be fun to create a Medical Guided Imagery script because you can easily encode a variety of symbolic messages that the mind-brain-body absorbs to change the internal function of the body. Although it is referred to as imagery, it uses all your senses and is experienced throughout the entire body not just in the mind. Medical Guided Imagery has been used in hospitals, medical facilities, and in private psychology practices for decades for a variety of health issues including for weight control, lessening the effects of chemotherapy for cancer patients, cardiac, diabetes, insomnia, anxiety, PTSD, depression, pain management and even in surgical centers for pre-surgery anxiety and suggestions for rapid post-surgery healing. NLP Neurolinguistics and Medical Guided Imagery is a powerful tool in mind-brain-body medicine used to communicate, instruct, and influence the function of the body

The Doorway To The Mind, Brain Body Connection

Your subconscious mind is the doorway to the mind-brain-body connection. The language of the subconscious mind is symbols, so you communicate with the subconscious mind through imagery, pictures and symbols, linguistics, or word phrasing used in the guided imagery script. The subconscious has no mechanism to determine real from unreal… an image is real to it.

The subconscious mind never shuts off, it is always taking in information and storing it in memory, even when you are unaware of it. When you sleep, the subconscious is dominant and when you dream in pictures and symbols, it is talking to you! That is why using imagery is so effective, it is the language of the subconscious mind, it is how you communicate with it, and how you instruct the mind-brain-body to effect change.

Tapping Into The Mind-Brain-Body Connection

When you are in a relaxed state, the conscious alert mind relaxes, opening the doorway to the deeper part of the mind, the subconscious and the mind-brain-body connection. The imagery of a warm sunny beach or any place you find relaxing can be used in the therapy script to relax the alert conscious mind, allowing the doorway to the deeper subconscious to open to the mind-brain-body connection.

There is a saying between mind-body behavioral specialist *"Where the mind goes… the body will follow" what you think and believe… is what your body will experience!*

Biofeedback & The Mind-Brain-Body Connection

Learning the NLP Neurolinguistic techniques in this program is remarkably similar to using professional Biofeedback therapy found in most medical centers. Biofeedback teaches you how to use the power of your mind to control bodily functions. Biofeedback is a machine with sensors that attaches to your body. The feedback teaches you to change or control your body's reactions to things by changing your thoughts, emotions or behavior, for instance, biofeedback can pinpoint tense muscles that are causing headaches and then you make deliberate physical changes in your body, such as relaxing the muscles to reduce stress and relieve pain. It has even been used to help prevent child bedwetting in children. In the same respect, when using it for stress control, you can learn to control and calm the functions of your body.

The ultimate goal is to learn how to use these mind-body techniques at home to achieve your wellness goals and reduce stress. NLP like Biofeedback is easy to learn, a typical biofeedback session lasts 30 to 60 minutes and most people see immediate results in habit change with NLP techniques. (Resource: Mayo Clinic mayoclinic.org)   Like Biofeedback the NLP Neurolinguistics techniques in this program will teach you how to control the function of your body and what you experience

The Lemon Taste Test

Studies show with a functional MRI (an MRI of a working functioning brain) that the brain cannot differentiate between what is real or imagined. It has no mechanism to do that. For example, when we envision a tart juicy lemon, our taste buds automatically begin to pucker up to the sour taste of a lemon even though it is only a thought or picture of a lemon in our mind. In the same regard the memory of a favorite childhood treat can make us crave or salivate in anticipation of eating the food. It has been proven that images of a dry, dusty desert will make someone thirst for water. The subconscious mind is tapping into its memory databank to trigger an action; like pucker up for a lemon or thirst for water.

In the same way, when using a functional MRI, if we were to imagine or view a picture of a relaxing beach, our mind-body begins to relax naturally and automatically. It uses memory, life experiences or perceptions. It associates a beach with relaxation. Our brainwaves will lower to a relaxed Alpha level when viewing beach imagery, which is the same Alpha level when someone meditates.

We really do not have to do anything, the subconscious mind does it all by itself, it knows what to do with the imagery by using memory, beliefs, and life experiences. If our surroundings are stressful, we can bring our minds to a place of calm by simply imagining a safe or relaxing place like the beach in our mind. The more you practice using a favorite place like a beach to relax and reduce stress, the more readily you will feel the results of the relaxation.

Practice Exercise: Lemon Taste Test

You can practice the Lemon Taste Test by simply taking in three deep breaths, exhaling fully, letting your muscles in your face, jaw and throat relax, relaxing your body fully. Then picture an image in your mind of a lemon, bright yellow, ripe, plump, and juicy lemon. See yourself carefully slicing the lemon with a knife and see the juice running on the knife and over your fingers. Breathe and relax again… Use all your senses, so you can smell the juice of the lemon, feel the juice run over your fingers. Now imagine taking a big bite out of the juicy ripe lemon. You can remember; you know the lemon is tart and sour. You pucker up, you can feel your taste buds pucker at the tart sourness of the lemon… just as if you really took a bite of the lemon. The Lemon Taste Test is an excellent practice for engaging the mind-brain-body connection through imagery.

Practice this technique until just the thought of a lemon triggers the puckering sensation in the body. You will be amazed at how easy it is to make this connection, how immediate and profound this connection can be.

KEY: Practicing the Lemon Taste Test helps to train your mind into quickly opening the door to the mind-brain-body connection. The more you practice this technique and ones like it, the more immediate and beneficial the mind-brain-body connection will be.

Exercise: Practice this a few minutes each day to open the doorway to the mind-body connection.
- Write down your first impressions of practicing the Lemon Taste Test. What did you experience? Sour taste, puckering taste buds?
- Is the connection more profound, stronger, more immediate with practice?

Module 4: A Revolutionary Technique To Heal Trauma

"The mind is released from darkness once we shine the light of a safe haven through touch" - Dr Ronald Ruden, MD

The Havening Technique

The Havening Technique (HT) is a new and revolutionary way to heal emotional disorders associated with stress and trauma. Disorders like depression, post-covid stress, PTSD, fear or phobia, anxiety, hypervigilance, grief, anger, resentment and the physical illnesses oftentimes associated with these disorders such as insomnia, digestive issues and unexplained chronic pain.

Havening was developed by two brothers Dr Ronald Ruden, MD and Dr Steve Ruden, DDS. Dr. Ronald Ruden studied how the brain encodes (stores) traumatic memory and how it acts upon the stored memory. The Havening Technique is a way to safely remove the negative affect of trauma on the mind and body without the person having to re-live the traumatic event.

Many people find it difficult to talk about traumatic events, with the Havening Technique there is no need to re-live or talk about the event. It may be difficult for some people to pinpoint specific emotions and for others there may be a sense of shame or guilt associated with an event that stops them from talking about the trauma to anyone. HT can help you release encoded (stored) trauma in a safe, gentle manner without talking about the event. It can be used in conjunction with any therapy, it compliments both traditional cognitive talk therapy and complementary-alternative methods of healing.

How Havening Works To Clear Trauma Symptoms

Havening sets off a neuro-electro chemical chain reaction in the brain which leads to a process called depotentiation or a dismantling of the stored trauma memory. Havening is unlike any other healing method; it deals with specific symptoms associated with a traumatic event encoded in the brain.

Havening will seek out the emotion associated with a specific encoded event that causes a specific symptom (depression, PTSD, fear, anxiety) and dismantles the link between them. Once the encoded event is found and dismantled the individual experiences relief of all symptoms. It can be a symptom associated with several events that is dismantled in one Havening session, thus releasing trauma symptoms from several events not just one. Havening has the power to release the root cause of the symptom completely and fully.

Remarkably after the Havening Technique has been completed to dismantle the traumatic memory there is no emotional connection to the event. You may or may not remember the event, but the traumatic response to the event is no longer present. Recall of the event no longer triggers emotional or physical symptoms

The Process of Depotentiation

The healing process that takes place with Havening is called depotentiation which breaks the emotional links associated with a specific traumatic event. The event can be completely depotentiated (**d**ismantled) without talking about the details. There is no pressure to talk or re-live painful events when using HT.

The Scientific Process

Learn more about the scientific process of Havening: Havening: a complete scientific explanation of the processes that take place in the brain to encode and the depotentiation of traumatic memory:
https://www.sciencedirect.com/science/article/pii/S1550830718301848

Havening Touch (HTT)

The Havening Technique uses the simple touch of your own hands in this amazing self-care treatment. Soothing gentle touch is applied to the arms, hands, and face. Through touch receptors in your skin HT produces special brain waves called delta waves which act directly on receptors in the brain where trauma is encoded (stored).

The Power Of Human Touch

Dr Ruden discovered repeated touch to parts of the body produces delta waves when combined with specific lateral eye movements (similarly used in EMDR therapy) and visualizations of something pleasant have a predictable effect on encoded feelings. The delta waves elicited by human touch are what enable a mother to comfort her baby and is hardwired in the brain of every person. Havening combines these deeply-seeded patterns of reassurance and comfort from human touch with sequences that breakdown unhappy feelings stored in the brain. This process elicits a rapid response, with just a few minutes of Havening, you should feel stressful emotions dissipate and experience calm relaxation.

Psychosensory Therapy

Havening Touch is considered to be a psychosensory therapy in the same category with EMDR (eye movement desensitization reprocessing), TFT (thought field tapping) and EFT (emotional freedom technique).

Psychosensory therapy is a form of therapeutic treatment that uses sensory stimuli (touch, smell, sight, hearing) to affect psychological and emotional well-being. It has roots in traditional Chinese medicine and with the latest neuroscience discovery in brain neuroplasticity it has found its place in neural retraining programs. According to the *American Psychiatric Association* (Journal 2016), psychosensory therapies are effective for treating mood disorders, general anxiety disorders, PTSD and depression.

All of these psychosensory methods are mind-body interventions used to make changes to encoded or stored emotion and thought patterns. You can self-haven or have someone else do the technique with you. If you have major psychological disorders it is recommended that you consult your doctor or therapist before beginning this or any self-care treatment.

A Clinical Study On The Havening Technique

A Study on the Havening Technique was published September of 2020 in the *Journal of Psychophysiology*. This clinical trial examined the impact of Havening Techniques on trauma responses in 125 participants. The study states there is evidence to the effectiveness of the Havening Technique creating sustainable long-term decrease in biological markers of stress and trauma while encouraging psycho-physiological resilience. Havening increases the levels of serotonin which can disrupt the consolidation of the link between the traumatic memory of the event and the distress that it causes.

The Havening Process Works Surprisingly Fast, Often One Session Brings Dramatic Relief

Use For:

- After a stressful or traumatic event (so event is not encoded)
- To calm "fight or Flight response in the nervous system
- To self-soothe, to reduce anxiety and calm yourself
- For insomnia, calm a racing mind to sleep better
- Stop worrying, stop renumerating or thinking about events

It Has Many Benefits:

- Clears a wide range of issues both emotional and physical
- No need to re-live or talk about the event
- Combines with other therapies
- Can clear symptoms associated with several events simultaneously in one session
- Permanent clearing of emotional connections to an event

It Can Relieve

- Anxiety
- Depression
- Fear and Phobias
- Grief
- PTSD
- Shock Or Trauma
- Anger
- Resentment
- Worry and Renumerating

- Chronic Pain
- Insomnia

It Can Be Used For Other Issues:

- Low self-esteem
- Confidence issues
- Self-image and perception
- Sport or work performance anxiety

Havening Resources

The Science Behind The Havening Technique

For the non-medical layperson, the scientific explanation of Havening is lengthy and may be difficult to understand. You don't need to understand the science behind Havening in order to perform the technique and reap the many benefits.

The following web links direct you to the scientific explanation (just in case you need that) and videos from Dr Ruden's website on how to perform the Havening technique. The technique has developed many variations and is now used for many other issues not just trauma.

Havening: a complete scientific explanation of the processes that take place in the brain to encode and de-potentiate traumatic memory:
https://www.sciencedirect.com/science/article/pii/S1550830718301848

Learn More about Dr Ronald Ruden Founder of The Havening Technique
Dr Ronald Ruden MD www.havening.org

You will find many variations of the Havening Technique that you may choose from. The videos on Dr Ruden's website and his YouTube Channel give you samples of the various techniques.

Videos of the Havening Technique by Dr Ruden
Videos (havening.org)

The Havening Technique

EXERCISE: The Havening Technique

1. Think of a specific event or stuck emotional block that you want to use the Havening Technique on. Do not re-live it, simply use your memory to recall what it feels like in the body. Notice how much discomfort, anger, sadness, fear, anxiety that you feel so you can rate it on a scale of 0-10

2. **Rate your Subjective Unit of Distress (SUD):** From zero to 10. With Zero being no emotions at all and 10 being extreme distress when you think of the event. Rating the distress gives you a starting point, as you perform the technique you will be able to compare the distress you feel after performing the technique and how quickly the rating decreases.

3. **The Eye Movement:** Keep your head straight and slowly move your eyes laterally from left to right and back to the left. Do this eye movement repeatedly as you do each step of the Havening Technique to the arms, hands and face. This specific eye movement produces delta waves in the brain. Delta waves are ideal for reprogramming the mind, brain and body and used specifically for neural retraining.

4. **Clear Your Mind**: Think or visualize something pleasant. You can imagine walking along a relaxing beach or magnificent garden pathway. If you are not fond of visualization, you can hum a happy tune like the happy birthday song. It is anything pleasant that emits a sense of joy, happiness and is calming. This step is not only meant as a distraction to the mind but is used to elicit brain chemicals connected to feelings of happiness that change the way the brain processes our thoughts and feelings.

5. **Start Havening - Arm Caress:** Clear your mind, breathe, relax and start the Havening Technique by crossing your arms in front of your chest, place your left hand on the right shoulder, your right hand on the left shoulder. Simultaneously with both hands, rub arms downward with a soothing caress to your elbows and then back up to the shoulders as you caress the arms

think of something pleasant like a walk on the beach, you can even hum a happy song like the happy birthday song if you like. While caressing the arms and thinking of something pleasant, you will use the side-to-side eye movement described above. Repeat this sequence of the downward stroke of the arms 20 times.

6. **Hand Caress**: Continue Havening by rubbing the palms of your hands together in a back and forth continual motion. Think of something pleasant and move your eyes from side-to-side. Repeat the back and forth movement 20 times.

7. **Face Caress:** Continue to apply Havening by gently rubbing your face with both hands. Across the forehead, over the eyelids, across cheeks. You may get an intuitive impulse to direct your hands to a specific area to caress. Think of something pleasant and move your eyes side-to-side. Repeatedly caress the face 20 times.

8. **Affirmation**: When you finish Havening, simply grasp your shoulders as if you are hugging yourself. Say a positive affirmation or word   (I am safe. I feel happy. I am healed. I feel strong)

9. **Rate Your SUD**:   Rate your SUD from Zero – 10. Has it lessened? Continue the Havening Technique until your SUD is zero.

While Havening and caressing the arms, hands and face, intuitively you may be prompted to caress your heart, your stomach or another part of the body. I always use the Havening Touch on this area as well. You may be amazed that you are prompted to caress the stomach and you have digestive symptoms or unexplained pain in the area you are prompted to caress. We know from the work of Neuroscientist, Dr Candace Pert MD that the cells in our body store emotions. You may be pleasantly surprised how an area of the body once tight, and tense will completely relax using Havening Touch sequence.

As you perform the Havening Technique or any psychosensory modality, other emotions, words or events may come to the surface. You may feel angry, sad, resentment, guilt, depressed, unloved, unworthy and others. You will want to Haven this feeling, word or event that surfaced as part of the therapy sequence to release the encoded emotions and trauma associated with this specific event. Use the SUD rating on each emotion or word that surfaces.

Important Note: Practice the Havening Technique before you read any further in the book. Begin the process slowly by using Havening on a minor issue; perhaps you are feeling stress from work today, frustration or sadness. Practice Havening for a few days on minor issues before you apply it for any major stressful events. Watch Dr Ruden's instructional video demonstrating the technique on his website (www.havening.org) and self-apply the Havening Technique as you watch his video.

Set Yourself Free With The Havening Technique

The Havening Technique heals trauma, but it also has the power to set you free from habitual negative thinking, lack of self-confidence and poor self-esteem that has previously sabotaged your personal goals. It breaks through mental blocks, dismantling the emotional block just as it dismantles encoded trauma blocks.

When you use Havening on mental blocks that sabotage your personal goals like procrastination, feeling unworthy or unmotivated, feeling unsuccessful or like a failure, it will automatically seek out and dismantle any encoded messages stored in the brain connected to these specific emotions, words or if there is a specific event that triggered these negative feelings.

When you use Havening on negative feelings you will be eradicating blocks and obstacles that sabotage your personal happiness. Havening empowers you to set yourself free and change your life.

Module 5: Techniques For A New You

Change Your Perspective… Change Your Life

This learning module is designed to help you regain the part of you lost from experiencing the stress or trauma. It will help train the brain for a new you, one that you desire.

Changing your perspectives is everything. When you change how you "see" or think about something including yourself, you change your behaviors to coincide with the new thought process or perspective.

The NLP Neurolinguistic technique of *Role Modeling* is used to change the internal image in the subconscious mind's master computer to forge new neural pathways for new beginnings, changing your self-image and changing your life.

The Power Of Changing Your Internal Self-Image

The way we see ourselves affects everything about us. You hold an internal self-image or perception about yourself that has been programmed into the subconscious mind's master computer. It is an outdated image suppressed by the stress and traumatic event. This internal self-image is what has been guiding your behaviors and habits.

KEY: When you retrain the brain, you are not only changing your habits and behaviors but as Dr Andrew Newberg's research has proven internal functions of the body will automatically change as well.

Role Modeling For A New You

We've all at one time had role models or wished we could be like someone. We wished we could play sports like an Olympian or have the success of someone like Tony Robbins. In the subconscious mind, Role Modeling connects an image to what you want to achieve. It gives the subconscious mind a blueprint to imitate and follow.

The key to successful Role Modeling is using a very vivid imagination to envision yourself successful, achieving a goal, being who you want to be, filling the vision with positive feelings and emotion. Remember, dream big and make that vision big, bold and wonderful.

The Foundation of Role Modeling

Dr Herbert Benson, MD, founder of The Mind-Body Institute at Massachusetts General Hospital in Boston Massachusetts was one of the first pioneers in mind-body medicine to use the Role Modeling technique in healing. Dr Benson used the NLP Role Modeling technique he called "Remembered Wellness" in his books *The Relaxation Response* and *Timeless Healing*.

Dr Benson discovered that the subconscious mind holds the blueprint of a person's perfect health in its memory. When faced with illness, pain or injury, the person can tap into the subconscious mind's blueprint of good health prior to any illness, injury or traumatic event, and it could return to that state of good health helping the person to heal faster. Dr Benson has successfully used this NLP Neurolinguistic technique on people with diseases, chronic illnesses, and injuries.

The 4R's System uses Dr Benson's "Remembered Wellness" technique in Role Modeling to trigger the subconscious mind to return to the blueprint of good health. In the master computer of your subconscious mind, we will be creating a new internal self-image of you, healthier, happier and free of stress and trauma using the Role Modeling technique. This will "Reframe and Retrain" the subconscious mind to a state of well-being, mentally, physically and emotionally.

You can use Role Modeling to achieve any goal, virtually for anything. Tony Robbins is a famous motivational speaker that teaches people how to be successful. He uses NLP techniques to reframe the person's perception of their ability to achieve success. Another example of Role Modeling is how Sports Performance therapists use it with Olympic Athletes where the athlete pictures themselves crossing the finish line, holding a gold medal, seeing their body perform at peak potential, believing they can be a gold medal winner.

You will learn the Role Modeling technique to change the inner image of yourself and your health held in the master computer of your subconscious mind. Your subconscious mind will use the imagery in the Role Modeling technique that you create for yourself to a new image of someone who is healthy, happy, confident and completely free of stress and trauma issues.

It is important when using Role Modeling technique that you use all your senses and make your new self-image very vivid, bold, strong and alive. You want to imagine yourself just as you genuinely want to be healthy, fit, active, happy… just as if you have always been.

A New Self Image

Think of Role Modeling as planting fresh seeds in the garden of the mind, where new perspectives will grow, you will find that once you change your internal self-image, a new way of acting, feeling, and thinking occurs naturally.

Practice Exercise: Role Modeling- Part 1

Begin this exercise by taking in several deep cleansing breaths and relaxing your mind and body. Get in touch with the natural rhythm of your breath and settle into the comfort of your own body.

- Use your imagination and picture yourself as you would genuinely like to be… healthy, fit, happy and free of trauma symptoms, chronic pain or illness. As is you never experienced these symptoms.
- Make the new image of yourself big and powerful, very vivid, as if you can feel it in every cell of your body.
- Make the colors bright and lively, see everything about yourself happy, well, successful and enjoying the highest potential of health and well-being that you can imagine.
- Evoke positive emotions feeling happy, confident and well with the new image.
- Picture this new image of yourself standing before you.
- Use your imagination and imagine you can simply step-into it… melt and merge with this new wonderful happy, healthy self-image. From the top of your head to the tip of your toes… mentally, physically, emotionally and even spiritually, you are this person.
- Now reaffirm to yourself that this is the new you, this is who you are.

Repeat this exercise three times in quick succession taking several deep cleansing breaths in between the imagery. Imagine you are installing a new software program in the master computer of your mind.

You will be using this Role Modeling technique daily. Each time you do this technique, the image should be more immediate, the feeling in your body changes, your mindset is happier. Use the same version of this self-image each time you practice this technique… enhancing the image and the feeling of wellness each time. Remember Role modeling is a tool used to reinforce new neural pathways.

Role Modeling has the power to build self-esteem, self-confidence and help you achieve personal goals in life. It's the beginning to regaining your life from the grip of trauma and a fresh start in life.

KEY: Remember the research of Dr Andrew Newberg mentioned in the introduction. Pictures, images, thoughts, words can change our perception of reality, from unreal to real. It can change the internal function of our mind and body.

The NLP Swish Technique

Dr Richard Bandler a leading scientist in mind-body development, created a powerful technique called "The Swish Pattern" that literally retrains your brain to easily change from one pattern of behavior to another, by "breaking" the habit. It releases old, outdated habits and behavior patterns.

The Swish technique actually causes new neuropathways to form in the brain or retrains the brain to easily accept a new realization or behavior. In regard to stress and trauma, it is that of a person healthy, happy and free of symptoms. Each time you practice the Role Modeling and Swish Technique together, you are retraining the brain to think and act differently. You are reframing in the mind what you will personally experience.

Think of this NLP technique as installing a new software package in the master computer of your subconscious mind that automatically conditions you to act, feel and think exactly as you have programmed this "new you." It uses the positive self-image you created in the Role Modeling technique above to help accomplish this.

Practice Exercise: The Swish Technique

This is a 2-part technique to release the "stuck" root causes of trauma (mental or physical), related symptoms, stored emotions, injury, chronic pain and illness. You will repeat the Swish Technique sequence for any trauma, injury, pain, symptom or personal behavioral habit you want to change. It incorporates the Role Modeling technique that you just used in the previous exercise.

- I want you to take one specific symptom or emotion that you want to change (like anxiety, worry, fear, sadness) and give it a symbol.
- Give this specific symptom any symbol that you choose, anything you want… whatever "symbol" pops into your head. (a block, a fire or flame, a hard rock, little gargoyle monster).

- Picture the symbol itself; feel it in your hand,
- Imagine you are holding the symbol in the palm of your hand.

Now let go of that image for a moment and put it aside.

- Get in touch with the new self-image you created of yourself in the Role Modeling exercise. Bring back the happy, healthy image of you that you created.
- Make the new self-image excessively big; powerful, it gets bigger and bigger, bolder and bolder, enormously powerful and strong in your mind. Do this until it is enormously powerful and strong. (yes, you can picture yourself as powerful as wonder-woman or super-man)

Now put this image aside for a moment.

- Once again, picture the symbol (gargoyle, fire, flame block) of the symptom you want to change in your hand.
- I want you to imagine that the big strong healthy image of you… is smashing the symbol of the symptom into tiny pieces or simply let it fade away. It is overpowering it and breaking it up into little pieces. (If you use the image of a fire or flame use a fire extinguisher to put the flame out. If you use a block break it into pieces or fade it away).
- Begin to clap your hands together repeatedly strongly (3-5 times). Imagine you are smashing the symbol in your hand into tiny pieces… until it is beginning to fade away. It gently fades away…. to nothing.
- With the count of 3… make the pieces smaller and fade the image of the symbol away to nothing… Count: 1- it is getting smaller, 2- it's fading away to nothingness, 3- it is completely gone now! Permanently gone! You are free of that symptom at last!
- Brush your hands off… gone. You can imagine washing your hands with clean water to get the pieces, dust feeling off your hands.

- You are training your mind and body to release the "stuck" old behavior pattern.
- Acknowledge how wonderful it feels to set yourself free.
- Now, reaffirm the big, bold, strong image of yourself from the Role Modeling.

Repeat both parts A and B exercises three (3) times in rapid succession. Then repeat it daily, you will know when you do not need to do this any longer.

KEY: The Swish Technique is life-changing and can be applied to any symptom, emotion, behavior or habit as well as any personality characteristic you would like to change. You will use the Swish Technique to release any trauma, injury, and on each symptom or emotion.

Adopt A New Mindset With Positive Affirmations

It is time to put your prior treatment failures behind you in the past where they belong. Do not let them rob you of your joy in life and new healthy mind and body. Adopt a new attitude of positive expectations with a "yes I can attitude."

Positive affirmations when said on a regular basis work to reinforce positive changes you have made in the subconscious mind. The work of Dr Larry Dossey MD has proven that our thoughts, beliefs, and spoken words are immensely powerful and can influence your subconscious mind thus creating an outcome or a reality that you choose.

Stop Self Criticisms & Negative Statements

It is important to remember that your subconscious mind is always listening… and it believes what you say. Your voice is immensely powerful. The subconscious mind responds immediately and without hesitation to your own voice. Stop negative self-talk, criticism and negative statements about yourself, your ability to control stress and start saying positive affirmations to reinforce your success.

Affirmations

- I have set myself free from stress and trauma
- I act and feel free of stress and illness. As if I have always been
- I have healthy habits and behaviors that support a healthy mind and body
- I have successfully released any old trauma (physical or mental) from the past… it is gone permanently
- I now have a healthy internal image of myself… as it is inside, it is on the outside.
- I now take loving care of my body, my health and my well being
- I deserve to be healthy and happy
- I am happy, fulfilled and joyful every day
- I feel more self-confident than I ever have before
- I can handle any stress that comes my way in a calm relaxed manner
- Stress bounces off me like a red rubber ball
- I sleep soundly and peacefully, awakening refreshed, energized and ready to start a new day

EXERCISE: write your own positive affirmation

Module 6: Control Stress and Build Resiliency

The Inner Sanctuary ~ Relaxation & Natural Stress Control

Stress and trauma were encoded in the brain because the landscape of the brain or lack of resiliency made you vulnerable to the encoding process. This learning module is designed to build stress hardiness, emotional resiliency and self-confidence in your ability to cope and manage stress.

You will be creating your own Inner Sanctuary to mentally escape, relax naturally and reduce stress. When you practice natural relaxation methods on a regular basis, you are creating a neural pathway of calm resiliency and inner strength. You can use this technique to help you sleep better and during times of anxiety to calm the nervous system.

You should practice the Inner Sanctuary natural relaxation method regularly to control the stress response in the body. I use the image of the beach in the Guided Imagery Script, so your subconscious mind automatically connects the image with relaxation. The Inner Sanctuary becomes your favorite place for escaping stress and a place you can go to relax.

The practice exercise uses Guided Imagery and the Progressive Relaxation Technique to relax all the muscles from the top of the head to the tip of the toes.

TIP: Record the Inner sanctuary part of the meditation script found at the end of the book onto your mobile phone for a 15 minute mini- stress buster. Listen to it regularly to build emotional strength and stress resiliency.

Practice Exercise: Create Your Own Inner Sanctuary

Use the beach imagery from the Recordable Meditation Script found at the end of this book to create your own Inner Sanctuary.

- Picture yourself walking along the beach and taking in all the sights and sounds, relaxing on the beach, going for a refreshing swim and feeling the warm sunshine.
- Record the progressive muscle relaxation technique to deeply relax the muscles from the top of your head to the tips of your toes! Remember to use the release technique "magical drains on the ends of your toes" to release stress, anxiety, negativity and any discomfort.
- Use the Role Modeling self- image, picturing yourself the way you truly desire, healthy, happy and well.

You create your own private escape. If you feel stressed, overwhelmed, having a difficult day… you will immediately use this technique to relax the mind and body.

If you practice this technique daily, you should feel the results quite immediately, as soon as you go to your Inner Sanctuary. You will be amazed at how quickly the "Inner Sanctuary" appears in your mind and you feel relaxation filling your mind-brain-body. By practicing this technique, you are programming your mind-brain-body for instant relaxation. Through relaxation, you open the doorway to the mind-brain-body connection. Through the mind-brain-body connection, you are in control of the master computer to achieve your goals.

The Stress Dial Technique

Each morning (and anytime throughout the day you need to) you will use the stress dial to calm your mind and body and eliminate stress symptoms.

- You will take 3 deep breaths… exhale and fully relax your mind and body.
- Picture in your mind the dashboard control center and the stress dial with numbers from -Zero to 10 with Zero being no stress and 10 being stressed out and overwhelmed.
- Locate your level of stress on the dial (or you may simply start at the number 10) and begin to slowly turn the dial down with each exhale of your breath.
- With your breath, as you exhale you are turning the number down. Your body is relaxing, muscles are loosening, symptoms are subsiding with each exhale as you turn the dial down to a lower number…until it finally is fading away. You feel calm and relaxed.
- Count down 10-9-8-7-6 breathe and relax with each number count 5-4-3-2-1-ZERO.
- You will repeat this up to 3 times until you have lowered your stress level to Zero.

The more you use this image, the more immediate and responsive your body will become.

KEY: Your body has no mechanism to tell it that this image is not the master control center for stress control. By using this imagery on a daily basis, you are creating a new neural pathway.

More NLP Techniques: Sub-modalities & Anchors

Using the new Neuroscience based upon the brain's neuroplasticity, it is flexible and has the ability to quickly "unlearn" behavioral patterns. You are tapping into the power of your subconscious mind to assist you in changing your own mental perceptions about your health and your ability to manage stressful events better.

NLP Sub-modalities

Sub-modalities: allow us to mentally manipulate a symbol to change it. We can use NLP sub-modalities to reframe or change how you perceive stress. You may feel consumed by anxiety, panic and fears. You may experience burning neuropathy pain and are given the symbol of a fire extinguisher putting out a burning flame (your neuropathic "hot" pain). You may describe your stress level as exceptionally large and all-consuming or hard and tough, you will use the appropriate sub-modalities to shrink it down in size, making it smaller until it fades and disappears.

NLP Anchors

Anchors: NLP uses anchors which can be symbol images or gestures to trigger a mind-brain-body response. Much like in the Lemon Taste Test… your body will respond to an image it knows in memory. A popular NLP anchor technique is when you press your thumb and forefinger together in an "okay sign," you can be given the suggestion that you will relax and be "okay" and free of anxiety when you make the "okay" sign.

 I like to use the Anchor of "water" as a natural relaxant so that the act of drinking water , showering, bathing, swimming in water triggers the body into a natural state of relaxation.

Water is a convenient NLP Anchor to use, and it is used for relaxation in the Recordable Therapy Script. I have given you the NLP Anchor of water in the therapy script; when drinking water, picture it is calming the nervous system, flushing toxins, rejuvenating, refreshing, energizing your body. Water is a natural relaxant; when drinking the water, you relax, can control stress and anxiety. When you drink water, it is an automatic mind-brain-body response; you relax automatically into a state of calmness. Imagine the water is like taking a magical pill that helps calm and relax you, it soothes away stress and anxiety.

My favorite is the NLP technique called The Dashboard. The dashboard is a powerful mind-brain-body control panel that has a variety of switches, gauges and dials with labels on them for relaxation, sleep, pain relief, vitality, energy… in the Recordable Script you will set these dials to the perfect setting to program or instruct your mind-brain-body for a given response. For example, when you turn off a light switch at bedtime, you can program your mind-brain-body for peaceful sound sleep. For stress relief, you are turning the dial down from 10-Zero until your mind and body is fully relaxed, stress completely fades away at zero.

Your subconscious is programmed to respond to these images… you can use them without listening to the entire mediation script by picturing the specific image you would like to use for example… take in a few deep breaths to relax, then picture the stress dial in your mind and start mentally manipulating the dial to a level of calm relaxation.

Finding Inner Peace

What does is inner peace mean to you? Everyone has an idea in their mind of what they think inner peace is. You want to be able to create this feeling of inner peace in your life without it being dependent upon other things like how a certain person acts, how your job is going or how certain life issues turn out. You can achieve this by simply changing your perspective, focusing on the positive rather than the negative.

Inner peace comes from within you… not from the things on the outside of you. The goal is for you to take inner peace and bring it to your outside world. You have the ability to do this by using the neurolinguistic techniques in this program.

You have the ability to change your perspectives on how you experience life. One of the ways to bring inner peace is to calm the mind… and calm the body.

Become mindful- You can create balance and stability by calming down and taking a few moments to think before you act.

Most people get so busy with their lives they forget to pause and check-in. Many of us engage in continuous motion, going from one thing to the next and the next without stopping. It is important to pause and take a mental break if you want to feel calm, stable, and balanced.

Stop and pause throughout the day, have a mindfulness moment, focus on what you are doing, change your perspective, quietly experience relaxation, a quiet mind brings a different level of awareness and inner peace. It can bring your emotions into a state of peace and quiet that becomes inner peace.

Steps For Quick Relaxation To Calm the Mind And Body

Natural relaxation methods elicits the relaxation response, which counter-acts the fight or flight stress response in the body. It helps naturally calm your mind and body. Some key symptoms of anxiety include tight tense muscles, shallow rapid breathing, worried thoughts and shaking. Natural relaxation methods target anxiety and its symptoms.

Breathe! Focus on breathing, calming your breathing is key to being calm and relaxed. Use a mantra or phrase while doing the breathing exercise to connect your mind and body with calmness…   "I am calm and relaxed"

Take 3 deep cleansing breaths… inhale through your nose… exhale through your mouth… just as if you are blowing out a candle… blow out all the air like a big sigh of relief… imagine calming your mind and body with each breathe.

…as you inhale focus on slowing down your breathing to a calm rhythm… exhale fully all the way down into your abdomen… releasing all of the air… continue to breathe slowly and calmly rhythmically…

You realize that you are getting all the oxygen you need, realize that your only job right now is to keep yourself as calm and comfortable as possible until the feeling of anxiety passes… fighting against the anxiety only makes it stronger so right now except that you are feeling anxious… and focus on calming your thoughts to relieve the anxiety…

Affirmations

Speak affirmations aloud to change negatives to positives

- I use the Havening technique to prevent encoding stress
- At the first sign of anxiety, I will take drinks of water... water has been programmed in my mind-body as my natural relaxant when I drink the water, I instantly feel calm and relaxed.
- I know that when I feel anxious that I am OK. The anxious feeling will pass, and no harm will come to me.
- I am safe even though I may feel frightened.
- I know how to make myself calm and comfortable while I wait for the anxiety to leave.
- I can help myself become gradually calmer and more relaxed by breathing calmly, thinking pleasant thoughts, and using the inner sanctuary imagery of my favorite place- the beach
- I give myself calm messages and I continue to breathe slowly in and out.
- I can walk around to get the adrenaline out of the muscles in my body.
- I am becoming calm and relaxed with each and every breath...
- I am calm and relaxed now.

Progressive Relaxation

Finally, focus on how to relieve anxiety by relaxing the physical body with the progressive relaxation technique you will find in The Recordable Therapy Script #1. Progressive muscle relaxation can help relax the physical body by releasing the tension held in muscles. Use the technique in the *Inner Sanctuary* section of the therapy script.

Self-Care: Building Resiliency

Resiliency helps you work through difficult times, it is the process of adapting in the face of an adversity, trauma or other significant sources of stress. Some people refer to resilience as "bouncing back from adversity" it helps you to move forward after difficult times.

Resiliency strengthens the landscape of the brain, so you are not prone to stress and trauma being encoded as traumatic memory. Doing activities that build resiliency like self-care activities, can prevent future episodes of PTSD or stress related symptoms.

One way of building resiliency is by practicing good self- care.

What Is Self-Care

Selfcare is a form of healthcare. It is not a luxury, and it is not being egotistical or selfish to take good care of yourself. When you have PTSD, depression, anxiety or any chronic illness, taking good care of yourself must be a top priority.

Developing a regular organized plan of Selfcare is essential to your overall health and well-being. In general, the goals of self-care are to find a state of good mental and physical health, reduce stress, meet emotional needs and find a balance in one's life. Self-care brings out the best in ourselves.

The benefits of Self-care are numerous. A regular program gives you emotional resiliency and can help you cope with life's daily stressors better. Self-care activities are empowering, it restores and replenishes your sense of well-being during and after stressful periods. It is an act of self-love, a form of compassionate healing for our own self.

It has been medically proven that when people participate in their own care program, it builds self-confidence in their ability to manage their health conditions better. It puts you back in charge.

I define Self-care as any intentional action that you take to nourish the soul and take care of your physical, mental, emotional and spiritual health. A Self-care program should be designed to fit your own personal needs. There is not any one-size fits all approach to developing a plan of care.

Self-care is as individual as we are. For people with chronic illnesses the plan is as individual as the illness we experience. What is soothing to one person may not be for another.

Some people find it overwhelming to take on too many new things all at once, start gradually with a couple of your top priorities to get the important care that you need and build on that. Health professionals often use the term self-care to refer to one's ability to take care of the activities of daily living, or ADLs, such as feeding oneself, showering, brushing one's teeth, wearing clean clothes, and attending to medical concerns but Self-care is actually much more than just ADL, it is nourishing the mind body and soul.

3 Key Selfcare Components To Whole Person Wellness

Modern selfcare nourishes the whole person, addressing your mental, physical, emotional and spiritual needs. It is simply taking the time to give yourself what you need. We all have different requirements for self-care and that is why it is so important to create your own personalized plan of care. You will find that the plan may need to be adjusted and changed over time to accommodate life changes.

You may focus your activities on ADL or basic activities of daily living while at other times you need to nourish the soul and feel pampered. Sometimes it will be about what you need right now in the moment. Plan self-care activities on a regular basis. You may find setting up a monthly plan by setting aside specific time in advance for activities works best.

Create Your Own Self-Care Plan

Start creating your own personalized Self-care plan by incorporating the things you love to do.   CAM Complimentary-Alternative therapies, walks on the beach, reading a book and doing your favorite hobby or craft can be a form of nourishing self-care. Anything that allows you to mentally escape stress is a good selfcare activity. It does not need to cost money, it can be a simple walk in nature or watching your favorite movie comedy that makes you laugh.

The purpose of the *Retrain Your Brain* series of books is to give you the tools you need to enhance wellness. Self-care regimens are an essential component to whole-person wellness.

You will learn powerful NLP Neurolinguistics techniques that promote wellness, natural relaxation and stress reduction in this book that can easily be incorporated into a Self-care plan. You can design your own plan that will soothe the mind, body and soul by using the stress reducing techniques in this book.

Exercise: Create a Selfcare plan for the week

Start your plan by asking yourself a couple of simple questions. You may want to start a self-care notebook and write your answers down on paper. These answers may change over time. Review your plan every three-six months or as you need to update it.

- What do I need most right now? Physically, mentally, emotionally and spiritually?
- What do I want?
- What will make me feel better right now?

If you feel setting up your own Self-Care program is overwhelming, you can find a variety of books and computer Apps available to help get you started on a regular plan of care.

Healthy Sleep

Getting deep restorative peaceful sleep is important for healing our mind and body. Deep REM sleep is a vital component to healing trauma.

If you suffer from insomnia, try natural relaxation methods like listening to the Recordable Meditation Therapy Script at bedtime for deep relaxation.

Retrain your Brain For Peaceful Sleep

Improving your sleep may require retraining your brain to fall asleep and stay asleep longer for sound restorative sleep. The Swish Technique found in this book can be used for insomnia to release the old behavior pattern of insomnia and pave a new neural pathway for sound restorative sleep. You can practice the Havening Technique before bedtime to calm and soothe the mind and body preparing it for peaceful sleep.

Good sleep behaviors may also play a role in peaceful sleep.

- Create the right conditions in a peaceful relaxed place that induces sleep.
- Control the lighting, most people sleep better in a dark room, filter noise so the room is quiet with no disruptions, a cool room temperature and a comfortable mattress may be key to solving insomnia. Some people sleep better with white noise; sounds of white noise, nature or ocean sounds while sleeping
- Develop a regular sleep routine: same time to bed, same time waking in the morning. Start a regular bedtime routine: where you give your mind and body time to wind-down from the day's stress or activities. Perhaps a relaxing bath before bed to relax the muscles and quiet the mind. Eliminate watching TV in the bedroom.

- Avoid caffeine, alcohol and cigarettes several hours before bedtime. If you go to bed after eating a big meal, digestive issues like acid reflux may be what keeps you awake.
- Manage stress so a worried mind does not keep you awake. If you are feeling troubled and cannot quiet your mind to sleep, try the Havening Technique before bed, start journaling to get the emotions out, keeping a gratitude journal by writing down the things you are grateful for in your life has been proven to help reduce anxiety and worry.
- Practice mindfulness meditation or guided imagery for sleep.

If you have tried natural methods and are still having trouble sleeping talk to your doctor for recommendations.

Exercise: Set up your own healthy sleep plan

1. What changes will you make to create a peaceful sleep environment?
2. What new sleep routine will you incorporate?
3. How will you soothe and relax the mind-body before bedtime?

Module 7: Cutting-Edge Therapy

About Recordable Meditation Scripts

Recordable Meditation Therapy Scripts are a breakthrough treatment in selfcare regimens. They are more effective than listening to pre-recorded audio MP3's and they empower people by taking an active role in their own wellness program.

Recordable Scripts Vs Mp3 Audio Downloads

Using your own voice in recorded scripts is the key to highly effective therapy. Listening to your own voice is more effective than listening to a pre-recorded MP3 download using a stranger's voice. Your subconscious mind knows your own voice. It recognizes and responds to your voice immediately, without hesitation, it accepts the symbols and suggestions as truth, as real because it is being instructed to do so by your own voice. It acts on the mind-body instructions without question. Your voice is extremely powerful whether it is used for positive affirmations or on your own recorded therapy audio. It results in quicker, more successful therapy outcomes.

How To Record The Therapy Scripts

You will want to read the entire book before recording the therapy script to understand how this therapeutic program can help you.

7 Easy Steps:

1) First: read the recordable therapy script aloud before recording it so you get comfortable with the wording and pauses (practice it before recording so you read it smoothly)
2) Set up your recording device (if using your phone turn the ringer to quiet)
3) Make sure the recording room is quiet with no outside noises so you will not be disturbed while recording.
4) Do a test for voice is at the right volume setting.
5) If you want relaxing music in the background, choose a soothing instrumental that has the right pacing to your speech. (You can purchase background music with just instrumentals to download online).
6) Read the script into the recording device, slowly, with a soothing voice.
7) When finished, save it, give it a title. (you may want to make a second copy in case the first gets deleted accidentally)

Recording Tips

Read the script completely before recording it. When recording the scripts, you want to use a calm, soft, relaxing voice. Talk slowly, use pauses to give yourself time to do the imagery and visualizations. Do not be afraid to make a mistake-read through and practice the script before you record it. I have capitalized some words you may want to emphasize while speaking. I use (…) to indicate a pause in the sentencing.

TIP: I like to use soothing instrumental background music on my recordings. I find it more relaxing.

Do Not Change The Wording Or Phrases In The Scripts

Do not add or change the wording, symbols, or imagery in the script. Do not shorten the length of the script. You may be changing the therapeutic outcomes. NLP Practitioners are trained in linguistics (wording), creating correct verbal suggestions or symbols that trigger the subconscious mind to take action by incorporating the correct symbols the subconscious mind will accept and act upon. The script is written by a professional and will have the appropriate NLP suggestions and techniques to help you achieve your goals.

Note: The only changes or customizations you should make is when using the mental checklist release technique in the meditation script where you are customizing the mental checklist of symptoms.

How To Use The Recordings For The Most Benefit

The scripts are meant to be read into a voice memo recorder like the one on your mobile phone so that you can have the convenience of using the recordings whenever and wherever you want.

The recordings are meant to be used in a relaxed, quiet setting where you can relax and daydream using the therapeutic images, symbols, and visualizations.

The best time to listen to the recording is at bedtime, where you simply drift off into peaceful sleep while listening to the recording. Do not worry if you fall asleep during the recording, it is more beneficial, remember your subconscious mind is most dominant during sleep and will absorb and act upon the suggestions more readily.

Listening to the recordings using headphones on a regular daily basis will bring the results you desire. Practice the NLP script techniques to pave new neural pathways to achieve your wellness goals. The more you repeatedly use these techniques the more effective and immediate the results will be.

Recordable Script 1: Healing Trauma

Recordable Script For Healing Trauma

Recordable script HEALING TRAUMA by Carol Charland
*All Copyrights Reserved 2021

Recordable Therapy Scripts are innovative therapy in neural retraining programs. The Healing Trauma script is designed to reinforce the work you completed using the Havening Technique to dismantle the traumatic event. It releases remnants of old emotions and symptoms related to trauma events. It does so without you re-living the event itself. It uses the Role Modeling Technique and the NLP Dashboard Imagery to fill in the gaps from the dismantling process with a new powerful self-image and positive mindset.

Use the instructions to record the scripts. Do not change the wording. Simply fall to sleep with the audio recording and let your subconscious mind absorb all the healing messages for a healthy, happy new you.

<u>START RECORDING HERE</u>   **(Read Slowly – With A Soothing Voice)**

NOTE: Please DO NOT Listen to this recording while driving the car of doing any activity that requires your alert attention. This recording can make you drowsy.

Begin by taking in three deep cleansing breaths and exhale all the way out into your abdomen. Simply relaxing and letting go with each breath that you take… let your body sink down into a relaxing comfort.

I want you to use your imagination and daydream, just as if you were on a wonderful vacation.

Picture yourself on a warm, sunny beach it can be any beach that you would like… it's a warm tropical place that you've always dreamed of traveling to… or a favorite beach that you've been to before-   use all your senses to place yourself in this daydream. Imagine the sights, sounds, smells…

This will be known as your "favorite place" it's your own *Inner Sanctuary* where you can escape to relax, let go of stress, tension, pain or discomfort.

Picture all the sights and sounds of this beautiful beach. Use all your senses to actually place yourself there -you can imagine yourself walking down the beach… feeling the soft sand on your feet… not a care in the world, stress-free, carefree and relaxed. With each breath you relax deeper and deeper… just letting your mind wander into the daydream. You can smell the fresh salt air… feel the warmth of the sun on your face… and there's a gentle breeze blowing through your hair… you see the crystal clear water with sparkling beams of sunlight dancing across the waves… it looks so refreshing… and you hear the rhythmic sounds of the waves as they roll into shore, in and out… the golden beams of sunlight on your face is so relaxing… you let yourself sink down deeper into the relaxation… all your muscles letting go… relaxing… it feels so good to relax… let go… escape for a little while…

Close your eyes… and feel the warm golden beams of sunlight on your face and body… sparkling beams of solar radiance… you breathe them in… and send them thru your mind and body… relaxing with each breath… breathing normally… easily… in and out…

I want you to imagine small, sparkling balls of golden energy… like beams of sunlight… you breath them in send them throughout your body… and as you exhale your breath… you are going to move the sparkling balls of energy…little beams of sunlight… thru your body… imagine that they clear a path… like a snowplow- plowing snow… clears away fatigue, tiredness, clearing away any old energy… old mental and physical stress, tension, clearing away any discomfort mentally, physically or emotionally… from the mind and body… clearing a path for new fresh energy… vitality… clearing and restoring all the energy pathways, meridians, to new… fresh life force energy and vitality.

Imagine the golden ball of energy like beams of sunlight are sitting at the very top of your head… With your breath as you exhale… you can move this warm flow of energy… golden beams of sunlight flow down over your forehead… relaxing all the muscles across your forehead… over your eyelids… and around your eyes… relax all the muscles in your face, it flows down into your jaw… and all the muscles in your jaw relax… flows down your throat … and it seems to flow right down into your shoulders… relaxing… flowing down your arms… clearing a path for fresh new energy… down into your wrist... and down into your hands and fingers… just imagine you can the warm flow of sunshine … flow right out through your fingertips… you are letting go of stress and tension… any pain and discomfort leaving your body… its clearing a path…

and you can feel that flow of warm golden beams of sunlight flowing down your chest… it surrounds your heart… it feels so soothing and comforting, loving… and it flows into your abdomen… softening the muscles… so warm and comforting… relaxing all the muscles in your abdomen…

as it flows down into your hips… down into your thighs… and legs… clearing a path… into your feet and toes… now, imagine that on the very ends of your toes there are these magical drains…

and you are letting this warm flow of golden beams of sunlight flow right out through the very ends of your toes… out through the drains… all the stress, tension, any pain or discomfort is leaving your body… as you relax more and more. Letting go… You can imagine yourself letting go of any stress or tension right out through those magical drains anytime that you need to… let your body deeply relax now… sinking down into the comfort of your own body.

Now… imagine those golden beams of sunlight filling your spinal column… like a golden tube of sparkling light… from the tailbone… the base of your spine… it flows upward… filling your spine… with healing energy… healing all the nerves in the spinal column… it flows upward… between the shoulder blades…up into the back of your neck… and the base of your skull… warm soothing, healing golden beams of sparkling light… you can feel that warmth relaxing all of the muscles in your back… in your neck… healing all the nerves in the spine… healing the Vagus nerve, the Central Nervous system… the Autonomic Nervous System… the Sympathetic and Para-sympathetic system… take a moment and see the spinal column… a golden tube of healing light… healing all the nerves… relax and absorb this healing light…

imagine the warm flow of sunlight moves up the back of your head… to the very top of your head… where it stays for a moment… the golden light surrounds your head.

your brain, your mental functions and emotions… its healing your emotional body… restoring mental function, clarity, focus, memory… you easily let go of any mental stress, mental tension…calming and soothing the brain… the warm soothing light simply absorbs it all… you feel clear-headed, brain-fog is gone… you easily focus… have mental clarity to make wise choices and decisions… all mental function is restored to normal…

Once again you can let that warm flow of sunlight flow down over your face… and it feels so warm, soothing, and relaxing…all the muscles in your jaw relaxing… It flows down into your chest and abdomen… just imagine that this golden sparkling light comes to rest in your abdomen… right above your navel… this is its home…

Just imagine you can throw out an anchor… grounding your energy… you feel safe, secure, grounded… centered and in complete balance… this is feeling of a deep inner strength… you can tap into it whenever you need to… you feel grounded, centered, balanced, secure and stable.

You've just made this complete circle from the top of your head to the tips of your toes… with little golden beams of solar radiance… restoring vital life force…

healing energy to the mind and body… you've brought this life force energy back to rest… in the abdomen… where it gives you deep inner strength…

You have just completed a technique for natural relaxation called *Progressive Relaxation* where you relax all the muscles from the top of your head to tips of your toes.
In Chinese-Taoist medicine this technique is known as the *"Circle Of Life"* moving life force energy to clear away old stale energy, any blocks to wellness, you are restoring the flow of natural vital, life-force energy that restores and heals the body… it automatically brings a renewed sense of health and well-being, fresh energy, strength and vitality. It strengthens your mind and body.

You can practice this breathing technique anytime that you would like… releasing stress, tension, pain or discomfort from the mind and body. You will always feel a deep inner strength… restored mind and body… and energized

Return to the daydream now… walking down the beach I want you to imagine that you can see the most perfect place to sit down and relax for a moment… I want you to picture in your mind a hammock… you're going to sit down and relax a while in the hammock… you can feel the gentle swaying motion of the hammock… it's so relaxing and soothing… as you swing back and forth… back and forth you feel the warmth of sunlight on your face… and you breathe and relax… stress-free… you notice the blueness of the sky above… there's some white soft fluffy clouds scattered across the sky… you relax deeper and deeper…

while you're relaxing in the hammock… we're going to begin to make a little <u>mental checklist</u> about stress … and any symptoms of stress that you may be experiencing.

This is just as if you are writing it all down on a list in your mind… it's a mental checklist

<u>First-</u> I want you to go back into your memory, I want you to write down on this list the stress or traumatic event. Do not re-live the event you are simply writing the name of the event on the list.

<u>**Next**</u>- I want you to write down on this list the <u>physical symptoms</u> that you have been experiencing in regard to the event. It can be physical like headaches, unexplained pain, fatigue, insomnia, digestive issues, allergies, muscle weakness, low immune function, brain fog or memory issues, perhaps you experience hyper-sensitivity to loud noises, bright lights, smells, or ringing in the ears.
 add any symptom you experience to the list.

<u>**Now**</u>- Write down any emotional symptoms like depression or mood swings, anxiety, fears and phobias, PTSD symptoms re-living the event, nightmares, hypervigilance or the busy mind that doesn't shut off, renumerating or worry, Add any <u>symptoms</u> to the list.

Add… any <u>feelings </u>like tension, feeling overwhelmed, grief or sadness, anger, anxiety, resentment, feeling unworthy…

add any emotional symptom – if you cannot put a name to a feeling you are having- just put a square box on the list… and label the box <u>unknown blocks</u> to represent this unknown feeling.

<u>**Now**</u>- you have everything you need on this mental checklist about the event. (don't worry your subconscious mind knows what needs to be there to help you achieve your goals)

<u>**Put the mental checklist aside for just a moment**</u>… and return to the daydream of the warm sunny beach… walking down the beach, relaxing. Breathe and relax… Taking in all the sights and sounds of your favorite place. Simply breath and relax for a moment….

At the end of the beach, you notice a <u>beautiful, hot-air balloon with a basket attached</u>- (you can make it be any color you would like) – the hot air balloon and basket is tied down to the beach with 3 silver cords.

Picture yourself standing in front of the basket of the hot-air balloon.

I want you to use your imagination… gather up the <u>mental checklist you just made about the event.</u>

That's right- picture yourself putting everything on the list into the basket.

- The specific event.
- All the physical symptoms
- All the emotional symptoms and feelings
- Ask your subconscious mind to add anything to the basket that needs to be there…
-

You're going to put all this stuff on the list… anything that has to do with the stressful event into the basket of the hot-air balloon… do it now.

<u>Everything… is in the basket that needs to be there.</u>

So, you can take a moment and breathe and relax… breathe in and out…calmly and easily

<u>NOW</u>- I want you to imagine… in your hand… you have a <u>pair of golden scissors…</u>

<u>You are going to cut the 3 silver cords… that holds the basket and hot-air balloon to the ground</u>.

Do that now! <u>Cut the cords.</u> Count #1… cut the cord. #2… cut the cord. #3… cut the cord.

All right- you did it… Good job!

<u>Watch</u>… the hot air balloon and basket float up into the sky…quickly and effortlessly up into the blue sky… there are some white soft fluffy clouds… a warm breeze is carrying it away… up higher than the clouds… and before you know it… it fades from your view… <u>and its GONE</u>. GONE permanently - never to return.

<u>Completely gone</u>… faded from your view. The hot-air balloon and basket has been carried away on that warm breeze… <u>never to return</u>.

So… you can relax now… your work is done.

Take in a deep cleansing breath and exhale all the way out… like a big sigh of relief.

<u>You have set yourself free</u>… from the symptoms related to stress and trauma. Your subconscious mind is going to use this simple <u>release technique</u> … to release and let go of any of the trauma or symptoms… from past or present… it has released any of the root causes of why you might have ever experienced it… and it does it immediately, easily and without hesitation…

You feel absolutely fantastic… you have set yourself free…

Trust that your subconscious mind knows what to do with the symbols, pictures and suggestions to help you achieve your goal

You don't even have to think about it… the subconscious mind knows what to do with the pictures and suggestions and releases it ALL… completely and automatically.

Now take a moment to breathe… imagine yourself basking in the warm sunlight on the beach.

You have set yourself FREE… that's right FREE… from stress or trauma and of the related symptoms…   It's simply gone!

Imagine yourself "jumping for joy" that's right go ahead… be happy… feel the freedom…feel the rush of excitement fill your mind and body… you have set yourself FREE!

You can now bask in that feeling of complete freedom… it feels wonderful…

Once again, return to the daydream… Imagine yourself walking down the beach… happier than ever before… joyful… you feel lighter… free, wonderful, happy… healthy… you are free of stress and any discomfort…   its simply gone.

Your mind and body will begin to immediately adjust to this new reality… free from distress or discomfort…   you feel happy, more alive, full of energy and vitality, more than ever before.

You return to a normal, healthy state… as if you have always been healthy. Remember Dr Herbert Benson's _Remembered Wellness technique_ Your subconscious mind holds the blueprint of your perfect health… you can return to perfect state of health and well-being… imagine that now.

(pause for a moment for the visualization)

(PAUSE FOR A MOMENT)

We will now use the powerful Role Modeling technique to instruct the mind-body

Now- I want you to go back in your memory and picture yourself before the stressful event.… before injury, pain or symptoms, before illness or disease.

Take a moment to get a clear picture… you can almost feel it… imagine the master blueprint of perfect health and well-being.

You can remember what it is like to be healthy and well both physically and mentally.

See the perfect image of yourself… from the master blueprint… age doesn't matter… it's the image and feeling you have of being healthy… that you remember… you know how to be healthy and well… and how to act-feel- and think in this way… as if you have always been.

Now use your imagination… you are on the beach… go back to your favorite place *The Inner Sanctuary*… feeling the warm sunshine, relaxing, daydreaming… walking down the beach…

And… right in front of you is the perfect image of you… just the way you a to be… in a fit, healthy body- emotionally strong, stress free and happy.

Next… I want you to imagine you can simply <u>step-into the image in front of you</u>…step into your healthy mind and body…

Imagine your body just melting and merging into this healthy image… from the top of your head down to the tips of your toes… down your arms to your hands and fingers… you melt and merge into the healthy body…   your subconscious mind knows how to do this…   it feels so real to you… because you are engaging your memory… it remembers this level of wellness… it knows how to do this… and it wants to do this… your mind-body wants to heal itself…   and now you have given it the tool to do so…

Take a moment, breathe and relax…   so, <u>you can feel this level of health</u>, wellness, life force energy returning to your body…   feel it in every part of your body, every cell, fiber, nerve, muscle… you remember… you know this feeling… its wonderful… you can really feel it… with each breath this sense of wellness gets stronger and stronger… you feel healthier and healthier in every way.

Make this new image of you big, strong, beautiful, make the colors bold and vivid… you feel so alive

Just breathe… relax and sink down into the comfort of your body… It feels wonderful… you remember… you know what wellness is…   you feel "whole" once again…   completely healed…

You relax and breathe… bask in the beautiful feeling… know its permanent.

Imagine the master computer in your subconscious mind…   you are deleting the old, outdated self-image and programming the master computer with this new strong healthy image of yourself…. Imagine flipping an inner switch… now lock it in place.

You now hold <u>the key</u> to the self-healing mechanism in your mind-body. You have unlocked the healing potential that we all possess…

You are in complete control… You take control of your own healing… your health and well-being.

Picture yourself holding a large golden key… you successfully have unlocked the healing potential of your mind-body… you are in complete control. You feel self-confident, empowered and you sense a deep inner strength… coming to the surface… it feels wonderful… you are taking back your life and can start living a full happy healthy life, where you can now achieve many goals.

The Dashboard: We will now use the powerful symbol of the <u>NLP Dashboard</u>- so picture in your mind a dashboard or control center and imagine this is the control center for your mind-body. You will adjust all the switches and dials to just the right setting to achieve your goals.

We truly do have a control center in our mind… and it is said… if you speak to the mind… the body will follow- we just need to give it instructions!

On the dashboard picture different gauges, dials, switches and knobs…

<u>The first dial</u> … you see is <u>a bright red</u>… it has a label on it that says…. <u>Stress and trauma</u>

The dial has numbers from 10 to zero. So the dial is set at 10… start to turn the dial down… you may even want to count to yourself as we turn it down to 9—let the stress fade away… 8—7—6 — you feel calm and relaxed 5—4 count down lower and lower turn it down fading any of the symptoms of stress to nothing… 3—2—1- and finally to 0—zero. Completely calm and relaxed, free of stress or trauma. Now lock it in place at zero.

Next, you will see a switch that has the label <u>Insomnia</u> (restless sleep) … I want you to turn that switch <u>OFF.</u> Just like turning OFF a light switch… when you turn your bedroom lights OFF… you are programming your mind-body for sleep. Telling it that at your given bedtime- it is time to sleep. Picture that in your mind now- when you turn OFF your bedroom light at bedtime you are instructing your body to fall asleep easily.

Affirmations For Peaceful Sound Sleep

- I fall to sleep easily at my given bedtime, I stay asleep throughout the night.
- If I should need to awaken during the night, I will do so… and handle anything I need to… And I will be able to return to sound peaceful sleep when I return to bed.
- I awaken in the morning feeling refreshed, well rested, and ready to start my day.
- I get deep sound peaceful sleep that heals my body, restores my health… and replenishes my energy.
- Each and every day, I notice how much better I feel… better and better in every way… healthier, happier and completely well.

<u>Next on the dashboard</u>…   There is a <u>green gauge</u> that is labeled <u>Health</u>… turn it to the high setting- <u>Healed and Healthy</u>. You have a high level of health and well-being.

Repeat to yourself 3 times- I am healed and healthy, healed and healthy, I am healed and healthy.

Next on the dashboard- picture a <u>dark blue dial</u> that has a label Anxiety <u>"fight or flight"</u> …   and I want you to turn that to the setting that says <u>normal.</u> Your sympathetic and para-sympathetic nervous system is in complete balance and harmony… it is normal.

You are naturally calmer and more relaxed now. You experience less anxiety.
You find you have healthy coping mechanisms… You easily find healthy ways to relax …naturally…

If you should feel any signs of anxiety… you simply take in 3 deep cleansing breaths and relax… with each exhale... like a big sigh… releasing any stress or tension… clearing your mind and body of stress

With the exhales… your mind and body relax…

You drink plenty of fresh water… you will find that water is a natural relaxant for you… when you drink water you feel calmer and more relaxed…   stress-free, any anxiety is washed away naturally.

See the <u>orange knob</u> that is labeled <u>Emotionally Resilient</u>… turn that knob all the way up to the setting that says <u>Deep Inner Strength</u> .

You are <u>emotionally strong and resilient</u>. You have deep inner strength that carries you through any situation… it does not matter what stress may come your way… you experience deep inner strength to cope and manage with life's ups and downs… you are emotionally strong… and resilient. You can now easily cope and manage with anything that comes your way… in a clam relaxed manner…

*Now… Lock it in place. Emotionally strong… deep inner strength.

On the dashboard there are <u>3 yellow switches in a row</u>… labeled Depression… Sadness & Grief … and Anger

Turn all 3 switches <u>Off</u>… just like turning off a light switch… turn the power off.

turn off depression. turn off sadness and grief. turn off anger and any negative emotion.

These negative emotions no longer have any power over you. Turn the power off. Lock it in place-- OFF.

There is one final switch you will turn <u>ON</u>— a beautiful pink colored switch labeled <u>Joy And Happiness</u>... the switch is the most beautiful of all the switches on the dashboard.

It is time to turn that switch <u>On!</u> Go ahead it's time for you to bring joy and happiness back into your life!

Imagine it's like turning ON the lights in a room where everything is brightly illuminated... it has a beautiful pink glow to it. Now lock it in place!

Take a moment... surround yourself with love, joy, happiness... like wrapping yourself in a beautiful rose colored bubble...   Picture the new life you will have with more love, joy and happiness in it...

<u>You Realize</u>... You have every switch, dial, gauge and knob on the mind-body control center- exactly where they need to be... to bring to you perfect health-- mentally, physically, and emotionally...

<u>Return to the image of the beach...</u> I want you to return to the daydream of the warm sunny beach... you are walking down the beach... you can see the crystal clear, warm water... it looks so relaxing and refreshing...

You relax... not a care in the world, stress free, carefree, deeply relaxed... just as if you were on a wonderful vacation...

you can imagine yourself soaking in the warm water as if you were in a bathtub... care-free, stress-free... so completely relaxed.

Imagine that you can feel the warmth of the water soaking into your body... into your muscles, into every fiber, tissue, nerve and into every cell. Its swishing and swirling... clearing and cleansing... detoxing the body... detoxing the organs...organ systems... it soothes and calms the nerves...restores and refreshes the nervous systems...

clearing away... washing, clearing every cell, fiber, nerve and muscle... flushing any blocks to your complete and total wellness... letting go... releasing it all... clearing cleansing... washing it all away.

Once again... imagine the magical drains on the very ends of your toes... the water flushes, clears and simply leaves the body thru these <u>magical drains on the ends of your toes</u>... until it gone. Completely cleared away...

I want you to now picture <u>a bottle of drinking water</u>... crystal clear, cool, refreshing... you like the taste of water and drink plenty of water... as you drink the water, it flushes and washes away stress... washes away symptoms of stress... clearing... cleansing... washes away fatigue and tiredness... washing way anxiety... as you drink the water... you feel calm, relaxed, refreshed... completely renewed.

as it clears away the old, it brings in the new fresh energy... fresh new vitality... energy... life force energy flows freely through your mind and body... restoring... refreshing... new vitality...new energy... health and well-being... mentally, physically, emotionally and spiritually renewed.

<u>You drink plenty of water</u>... you keep your body well hydrated... when you drink the water you are stress free... you feel calm and relaxed, free of anxiety, ...
you are full of energy and vitality... you remember to drink the water.

Your subconscious mind now uses the symbol of water to clear and cleanse your mind and body... when you drink the water you are free of stress...

When you drink the water, you are...free of anxiety, you feel relaxed, calm, refreshed and restored of vital life force healing energy.

Your subconscious has been given the symbol of water... it is your natural way to relax... stress-free calm and relaxed when you drink the water

---

Take a moment and practice Role Modeling Technique again... only this time picture your life the way you would like it to be... (pause for as long as you like to imagine your heart's desire... the future you want for yourself where you can see yourself successful... financially prosperous... healthy...
everything you always dreamed of...) Get a clear image...

NOW... Imagine yourself stepping into this new you- into a new life! The life you have always dreamed of having. Your heart's desire.

Spend as much time as you like basking the imagery you have created.

Picture yourself once again walking down the beach... use all your senses to place yourself in this favorite place you have created... this is your inner sanctuary... a place of healing... a mental escape where you can go to relax whenever you choose... by simply breathing... relaxing... and using your imagination to daydream... your subconscious mind knows this place... this healing sanctuary you have created.

You have finished this healing therapy, you might not understand exactly how all of this works... but just know that your subconscious mind... the most powerful part of your mind... knows what to do with the healing suggestions, the symbols and images that it has been given to heal your mind and body.

The more that you consistently listen to this recording, the more powerful the healing is. Your mind and body respond to the healing images, techniques and suggestions to return you to perfect health. You are healed and healthy today and from this day forward...

(Read This Next Section In A Louder, Stronger, Commanding Voice)

You Will Now Awaken And Return To Your Alert State Of Mind –

Open Your Eyes On The Count Of 3

Open your eyes and begin to awaken… be alert… Come back into your surroundings… and your body… On the count of 3- you will be wide awake and alert.

---

1.   **Open your eyes and be aware of your surroundings**
2.   **Feel awake. in your body… sit up and move your body**
3.   **You Are Wide Awake And Alert Now-   wide awake and alert…**

(PAUSE AND READ *if this is your bedtime… you will be able to put the recording away… and return to peaceful sleep, awakening in the morning at your given time feeling well rested, energized ready to start your day… completely free of pain or discomfort)

<u>THE END OF SCRIPT</u>

Personal Notes For Script #1 :

Recordable Script 2: Building Strength & Resiliency

Recordable Script For Building Strength & Resiliency

Recordable script Building Strength & Resiliency
by Carol Charland   All Copyrights Reserved 2021
Medical guided imagery Script designed to build inner strength, resiliency and coping mechanisms

Recordable Therapy Scripts are cutting-edge therapy in neural retraining programs. The Building Strength and Resiliency script is designed to help you build emotional strength and resiliency for coping with everyday stress.

Use the instructions to record the scripts. Do not change the wording. Simply fall to sleep with the audio recording and let your subconscious mind absorb all the healing messages for a healthy, happy, more self-confident new you.

A Mountain Of Strength

DO NOT Listen to this recording while driving the car of doing any activity that requires your alert attention! This script is designed to help you daydream and relax, it can make you drowsy or sleepy!

This is a sitting meditation designed to help you weather life's ups and downs, manage stress, build inner strength, emotional resiliency and healthy coping mechanisms.

To Begin:

Sit up-right in a comfortable chair or couch with your feet on the floor to practice this meditation. Choose a place where it is quiet, where you can relax, close your eyes, daydream and not be disturbed. (10 minute mini-script)

(START RECORDING HERE)

We begin by taking in several deep cleansing breaths… breathe in through the nose and exhale fully through the mouth…   Bring your attention to the flow of your breathing… calmly, rhythmically… in and out… feeling each breath…

gently in and out…. just focusing on your breathing… allow your body to relax with each breathe… feel the muscles relaxing… just bask in the stillness… quiet and relaxed.

I want you to begin to use your imagination… to daydream… imagine yourself now as you're sitting upright… that you're sitting with a sense of strength… power… a sense of resolve… a sense of being complete and whole… let your posture adjust… your spine is straight and strong… your posture sitting in the chair is reflecting a sense of strength power…

Now I want you to imagine… the most beautiful mountain that you have ever seen… perhaps it is a place you have been to before… or a magical place you create in your mind… imagine a majestic powerful mountain peak… begin to get the sense and feel of this mountain…   you can see the overall shapes of the mountain… high peaks that reach up to the sky…

A large solid base of the mountain is rooted in the strong rock of the earth's crust… so majestic and powerful… it has some gentle sloping sides to the mountain… but you can see and feel how massive it is… how solid… unmoving… strong and beautiful it is.

Perhaps your mountain has snow at the top… trees… maybe one prominent peak or high plateau… whatever you would like it to be… you are relaxing… just sitting and breathing with the image of the mountain…
You can see all sights and sounds around the mountain… the blueness of the Sky… white soft fluffy clouds floating by… notice the sun is shining… the brilliance of the sunlight shining… a warm solar radiance beams strands of sunlight down to the Earth…

You relax just breathing in the warm beams of sunlight… sending it through your body, warming, relaxing, melting into the sunlight… relaxing all the muscles on your face… across your forehead… relaxing the muscles around your eyes and eyelids… and you can close your eyes…. And you relax deeper and deeper now… letting go of stress or tension…

Let the warm flow of sunlight flow down your face… into your jawline… relaxing the muscles of your jaw… down your neck… throat and chest… into your shoulders… down your arms…. Into your wrists… hands… fingers… right out thru the tips of your fingers…

Now send the relaxation flow down your spine… relaxing the muscles in your neck and back… your hips… and into your abdomen… down your legs… into your calves… feet… and toes… wrapping your body in this warm soothing comforting light… melting into relaxed comfort. Completely relaxed…

Go back to the image of the powerful strong mountain that you created… imagine you are there standing in front of the mountain… gazing at its majestic strength… breathing in the awesome power…

Imagine as you breathe in… you can bring the strength of the mountain into your own body… so that as you sit upright in the chair… your body becomes one with the mountain… you become the mountain rooted in your sitting posture… your head becomes the lofty peak supported by the rest of your strong body…

Your shoulders and arms are the sides of the mountain… your buttocks and legs are the solid base… feel the strength building up in your legs… your feet are grounded in the Earth at the base of the mountain… you can feel the strength of the mountain coming up through your feet… up into your legs… up into the base of your spine… to the very top of your head… it brings deep inner strength into your mind and body. Take a moment and sense and feel the strength… the power within you now.

You feel uplifted… straighten your body… you are sitting up straight… strong… you can feel the strength building up in your physical body… your spine is strong and straight… and with each breath as you continue sitting… you become more and more like the mountain… stronger, physically stronger… unwavering in your strength… there is this deep inner strength from the base of the mountain that you feel surge up into your own mind and body… you have more physical strength… you feel mentally and physically stronger than ever before…

You feel this unwavering strength it is who you are now… picture an image of yourself in your mind… imagine stepping into this strong mind and body.

It is a feeling that goes beyond words… with a simple thought… you feel deep inner strength… centered… rooted… grounded…a strength that is deep within you now… that seems to grow stronger and stronger… like the trees on the mountain… it feels wonderful to be mentally and physically strong and well…

Now you are becoming aware of the fact… that as the sun travels across the sky …the colors in the sky are changing… virtually moment by moment… night follows day… and day follows night…

There is a canopy of stars… you can see the moon… the sun… and through all the changes the mountain just stays forever strong… through all sorts of weather… the mountain weathers the storms… yet the mountain remains strong with resolve… it is constantly able to cope with any changes that comes its way… it always remains strong.

It can handle anything that comes its way… and remain strong mentally and physically.

You are like the mountain; mentally and physically strong, imagine you can wrap yourself in the strength of the mountain, mentally, physical, and emotionally it brings you healing, health and wellness.

The seasons can come and go but the mountain remains strong… and like the mountain… you have a deep rooted strength… a deep inner strength… you can handle any stress that comes your way in a calm, relaxed way…

You have natural, healthy coping mechanisms that keep you strong and resilient… you are emotionally strong and resilient like the mountain… you have a deep inner strength that can get you through any storm… just like the mountain.

In summer… there's no snow on the mountain except perhaps for the very peaks… in fall the mountain may wear a coat of brilliant fiery colors… in winter a blanket of snow… in any season it remains strong… it may find itself shrouded in clouds or fog… pelted by rain… people may come and go… the mountain remains strong… solid… and beautiful… none of this matter to the mountain   which always remains its strong self… grounded… rooted in strength…

Clouds may come and go… the mountains magnificence and beauty are not changed one bit by the way people see it… not by the weather… not by anything seen or unseen… The mountain weather the storms … in a tower of strength.

And in the same way, as you sit in this meditation… you are the mountain… you embody the same unwavering strength… emotional resiliency… majestic calm peacefulness… you are rooted in this massive strength from deep within… that in the face of everything that changes in your life… you are still strong and resilient…

and like the mountain... in your mind... and in our body... you may experience changes but just like the mountain you stay strong.

Through any stress, life crisis or illness... you cope and manage... you remain strong like the mountain.

You will remember... be like the mountain... sitting strong... posture straight... feet grounded in the Earth... you have a strong resolve and deep inner strength... you can handle any stress that comes your way in a calm relaxed way... stress just bounces off you... you have healthy coping mechanisms that keep you strong and emotionally resilient... just like the mountain. You are a mountain of strength.

You can handle any stress that comes your way in a calm relaxed way... no matter the season... no matter the life changes... you can embody the same unwavering strength... relaxed calmness... deep rootedness... you are the mountain... in the way you act- feel and think.

When you stand up, you feel your feet rooted in the Earth, the strength comes up into your legs and body... fortifying you. You feel the strength in the muscles of your body... in the sense of vitality and life force energy.   You are mentally as strong... you are stable, feel secure and safe.

Now...   take in some deep cleansing breaths... and relax... sink down into the comfort of your own body and just acknowledge this blissful state of complete relaxation for a moment before we end this meditation...

You can feel the strength and power that you have brought into your mind and your body... into your emotions... you have the strength... resolve... power and wholeness once again... your mind, body and spirit heals itself... you are the mountain... forever strong.

If you feel under stress... overwhelmed... in need of strength to cope... if you need deep inner strength... you will simply breathe in and out... picture the mountain in your mind... sit down and ground your feet into the Earth... feel the mountain coming into your mind and body… bringing the strength you need to handle anything that comes your way…

(read in louder more commanding voice)

On the count of 3… you will be wide awake and alert… feeling an awesome powerfulness and deep inner strength

Number 1… open your eyes and feel wide awake and alert.

Number 2… move your body… feeling fantastic and energized

Number 3… completely wide awake and alert   Wide awake and alert-

<u>THE END OF SCRIPT</u>

Module 8: The 14 Day Plan For A New You

The Trauma Survival Tool Kit

The book is divided into learning modules and offers a step-by-step teaching guide to practice the NLP Neurolinguistic techniques. You can create your own customized self-care program by utilizing this plan. Start by priority.

Below you will find the priority steps to getting started on this program:

- Priority 1: Use the Havening Technique to dismantle the traumatic event and related symptoms. Practice the technique as instructed until the symptom is eliminated.

-

- Script 1: Read through the Recordable Meditation Therapy Script and set up your recording device to record it so you can begin listening to it immediately. Record and listen to the Recordable Meditation Therapy Script recording for 7-14 days. Listen to Script 2 as often as you would like to build inner strength and resiliency. Simply fall to sleep listening to the audio recording and let it fill your mind, body and soul with the healing messages. After the 14 day period, listen to the audio recordings a few times a week then perhaps once a month for maintaining the changes you have achieved.

-

- Role Modeling Technique for a new you. Practice the visualization on a daily basis

-

- The Swish Technique: Start using the Swish Technique to release unwanted personal habits, stress, pain and symptoms. You can use it for stress and anxiety or any behavior pattern you wish to change. You may want to record the step-by-step guide to the techniques, so you automatically follow each step of the technique. Repetition of these exercises is key to successfully paving new neural pathways for change

*

* Stress Control: Record *The Inner Sanctuary* and *Progressive Relaxation* part of the meditation script 1: listen to it for regular relaxation and stress control. Use it whenever you feel stressed, anxious, or overwhelmed. It can be a short 15 minute stress buster that helps calm the nervous system.

The 14 Day Journal

Document your progress on each of the 14 days of the plan. Keep a notebook of your activity and progress. You can use the note pages to journal about your progress, express emotions, set new goals and list any achievements.

The Havening Technique

The specific event used for Havening is: _______________________

- Record your SUD numbers before and after applying the Havening Technique.
- Record the symptoms, emotions and words used to clear stress and trauma
- Document changes you have experienced.

Record Noticeable Changes:

1. List new things that has changed about myself, my personality or self-image
2. List positive changes in my health. Physical and emotional.
3. List coping mechanisms or how I cope better with stress.
4. List positive changes in my life (new job, relationship, better sleep)

List Self-Care Activity: ____

List Stress Control Activity: ____

Journal Writing Prompts

Today I did something I always wanted to do… (Finish the sentence.)

Today I am grateful for…

Tomorrow I will achieve…

A Final Note From The Author

The strategies in this book differ from the mainstream approach for the treatment of stress and trauma. As you begin to implement the program and practice the techniques, you will find some may have an immediate impact on reducing your symptoms while others may take a bit longer to integrate.

Do not give up prematurely! Complete the program as instructed, repetition to create new neural pathways is key to your success. If you complete the program as instructed at the end of the 14 day period, you should notice a remarkable difference in your ability to self-manage stress and you may find the symptoms related to stress and any trauma once thought to be unchangeable, may be eliminated entirely. Continue using the program until you are able to reduce the symptoms entirely.

I have seen people, and also experienced myself, that by using *Retrain Your Brain* methods, you can rise above the negative effects of stress and trauma, PTSD and even chronic pain in an amazing way. When I used the techniques to release the old stuck pain trauma messages, it changed how I experienced CRPS pain, and my entire life changed for the better. I am now in a state of remission.

You too can be more productive, can enjoy life once again and you may even find a new life purpose as I have in writing the *Retrain Your Brain* series of wellness books.

You will find that once you master the NLP Neurolinguistic Techniques found in this book, you can use them to achieve many other life goals that can help increase your overall joy and happiness in life.

I hope this will only be the start to a positive new beginning in life for you.

About Carol Charland

Carol Charland holds a Diploma in CAM Complimentary ~ Alternative Medicine, she is a NLP Neurolinguistics Practitioner specializing in pain management and a Certified Clinical Hypnotherapist since 1998. She is a member of IACT, The International Association of Counselors and Therapists.

Carol developed the revolutionary new 4R's Neuro-Healing System based on the latest discoveries in Neuroplasticity training. She offers a variety of *Retrain Your Brain* wellness books, courses and private coaching programs via Zoom online.

As a Pain Management Practitioner, Carol has a unique understanding of persistent pain, better than most author-therapists. She has CRPS- Complex Regional Pain Syndrome rated the highest known pain syndrome on the McGill Pain Scale. She knows the struggles of living a life in persistent pain. She has written the therapeutic pain relief programs not only from her expertise as a CAM Pain Management Practitioner that has successfully helped hundreds of clients over the years but also from her own life experience of living in persistent pain.

Carol lives in beautiful Southern Coastal Maine. She enjoys time with her grandchildren and the beautiful Maine beaches, mountains and lakes where the motto is "life the way it should be." When Carol is not writing, she loves to walk the beach with her little diva canine, Daisy collecting sea glass that has washed up on the shores from around the world.

Retrain Your Brain Series

The Retrain Your Brain Series For General Wellness

Healing Trauma
Stop Smoking
Weight Loss
Stress Control
Freedom from Anxiety, Panic and Fears

The Retrain Your Brain Series For Pain Management

There's Life Beyond Pain

The Pain Management Series Is Written Specifically For:

Fibromyalgia
CRPS
Lyme Disease
Neuropathy
Shingles
Reynaud's Disease
Gout
Spinal back and neck pain

Acknowledgements

Writing this series of wellness books has been an extraordinary experience that has changed my life for the better in so many ways. It has been a lifetime dream of mine as a CAM therapist to author a book that will help lessen suffering for people all over the world. I am grateful for the many blessings it has brought to my life.

- To my family, friends and therapy clients: Thank you for your support and encouragement in publishing my work.

- Patricia Wilson: Proofreading & Editing Services

- Hollie Anne Marsh: Marketing Services

- Indie Group: Book cover layout for paperbacks

- Katherine Mayfield: For her motivation and expertise in helping me become an Independent Author and Publisher. Katherine is the Author of the award winning memoir *"The box of daughter; A guide to recovery from bullying"* and *"Stand your ground: how to cope with a dysfunctional family"*

Personal Notes: